ANCHOR BOOKS

Celebrations In Words

Edited by

Simon Harwin

First published in Great Britain in 2003 by
ANCHOR BOOKS
Remus House,
Coltsfoot Drive,
Peterborough, PE2 9JX
Telephone (01733) 898102

HB ISBN 1 84418 223 1
SB ISBN 1 84418 224 X

FOREWORD

Anchor Books is a small press, established in 1992, with the aim of promoting readable poetry to as wide an audience as possible.

We hope to establish an outlet for writers of poetry who may have struggled to see their work in print.

The poems presented here have been selected from many entries, and as always editing proved to be a difficult task.

I trust this selection will delight and please the authors and all those who enjoy reading poetry.

Simon Harwin
Editor

CONTENTS

Ruth

How happy I was that cold January morn
When I gave birth to my first born.
Oh, how my heart when all a whirl
When the nurse declared proudly, 'You've a little girl!'

You were so tiny, pretty and very sweet,
And with pride I examined you from head to feet.
There was not a blemish that I could find
As I checked your fingers, toes and small behind!

I gazed at you as you laid there, so very small,
Wrapped up tight in that white hospital shawl.
You puckered your little lips and opened your eyes,
They were blue like the ocean and clear like the skies.

I brought you home, my bundle of joy,
And rearing you I did so enjoy.
Pushing the pram was such a treat,
I had the prettiest baby in the street.

With your lovely face and auburn hair
You were a cute little girl with masses of flair.
At school you worked hard and did excel,
And at home we always got on so well.

And now that baby of mine, that was so small,
Has grown into a lady, but not so very tall!
She still has those blue eyes and auburn hair,
Her many fine qualities and still that flair.

I'm as proud of you now as I was before,
I enjoy your company and would like to see you more.
To me you are the perfect sample -
I thank you for setting such a good example.

Glenda V Llewellyn

Verse Must Celebrate

Do you often wonder what is worse
Than finding a card without any verse?
The birthday of a friend or mother,
That anniversary of your sister or brother,
You have to mark that special celebration,
But finding the right card brings aggravation.
Something so nice can't be too tarty,
Put on a gift you take to that party.
Don't care about the cost or worth,
Real verse is like all the gold on Earth.

In poetry it is a century of crime
You find a card without even a simple rhyme.
What are we poetry lovers ever to do,
All cards will only make folk feel blue.
Do publishers of cards need any excuse
To all kinds of verse just mass produce?
Bring back those happy words of joy,
Come on firms, make Colin a very happy boy.
I have been looking for that card for hours,
At last Forward Press use their magic powers.

Colin Allsop

Wedding Anniversary Ode

You are my sun and moon and stars,
my Venus and my Mars;
you are my rest of outer space.
But all of this can never be
enough to house my love for thee.

Edward Fursdon

Writing's A Tonic!

W riting's a tonic, yes, indeed!
R elaxing to the mind!
I n times of stress, in times of need,
T o help you to unwind!
I n truth, the pen is mightier!
N o doubt at all in this . . .
G od knows our meanings must be clear -
S uccinct won't go amiss!

A gentle word, a piece of prose,

T riumphant themes and more,
O pinions sought, meant to propose,
N ot easy to ignore!
I 've done my part, this much is true . . .
C alligraphy's now up to *you!*

Denis Martindale

The Eighth Of May

I wed in May, a girl so gay!
You took as wife, me and my life!
A flower grown that you did own.
I'd no regret, the stage was set,
We stood as one before each other.
Now forty years have passed us by,
I'm looking back, I'm wondering, why?
Would unwed we have stood
So many years of love and pain
And found another life the same?
It ended long ago and yet
I'd live again, the stage was set.

Joan E Blissett

THE NEW BEGINNING

When a baby is born
His mother forgets the anguish and pain
That she has had to go through,
So that new life can start again.
For that one glorious moment
When she holds new life in her arms,
Makes all the struggle of carrying that child
Worth it. Birth and death are similar in some ways -
Birth is the opening of the door,
And death is closing it . . .

When a baby is born
Both parents are glad.
'So long as he is healthy,' say the proud mum and dad.
This fragile little being, who cannot do a thing,
Without the help of his parents,
Except cry and fret when he is hungering.
This tiny little infant, smells so fresh and so new,
And responds to closeness and comfort from only a few.
So much joy this baby brings,
With cards, teddy bears and miniature clothes and things.

When a baby is born
A new world opens all around.
Beginning with nurses and doctors in hospital,
The infant responds to love and care,
And beauty, from sights and sounds.
After he goes home to be with his family,
A little personality develops as he grows.
He changes day by day, week by week, for all to see.
Emerging into a special child that everybody knows,
He is happy, healthy and free.

Hilarie Grinnell

Life's Landmarks

Give thanks for celebrations,
The landmarks of our lives,
They raise our spirits when they're low,
And families unite.

Life starts as celebration,
Rejoicing at a birth,
A sign of hope and future joy
For parents, friends and kin.

The toddler's first unsteady steps,
Achievements in school days,
A working life brings more success
And lasting friendships forged.

A marriage celebration next
When joy is unconfined,
Another birth, or two or three,
New generations come.

Sweet anniversaries will mark
The passage of the years,
The happy times at work and play
Until retirement comes.

The evening of our lives will bring
A time to sit and muse
Upon the celebrations shared
Along the road of life.

Death comes to everyone at last,
But sadness need not be,
For all should celebrate with love
A life that's been well spent.

Roma Davies

For Georgia

Spring came rather early in 1953
Saturday 14th March was a special day for me
A day of great importance, unlike any other
For on that long-awaited day, I first became a mother
Georgia announced her arrival - as only Georgia could
And the family all adored her, as all our family would
Since that day, I see her - my pixie daughter dressed in flowers
With a smile like summer sunshine
Brightening up the hours
You have made me so very proud of you
And all the things you've done
I hope your cherished dreams come true
Each and every one
May you always find great happiness
With friends who love you most
Please count me in as one of them
And to this I raise a toast
For no matter where I go I find
Georgia's always on my mind.

Nancy Sheldon

A Golden Wedding Day

Life is like a journey as we travel down the years,
Many paths that lead us through happiness and tears.
But when you are with that someone who is always by your side,
Then life is just so wonderful when love becomes your guide.

It hardly seems believable that now it's fifty years,
Our wedding day and the vows we made, still remain forever dear.
Blessed were we when family came, a girl and then a boy.
They have been so good to us and given us both such joy.

The journey we set out on has still a few more bends,
But true love never falters and will be with us when life ends,
This happy day has prompted me to write this poem for you,
And what better way to finish, than say, 'I love only you.'

Margaret Findlay

NANNIE'S PRIDE

Ten tiny fingers, ten tiny toes,
Two sparkling eyes and a button for a nose.
A perfect little head with shiny, silken hair,
Loved by all who meet her, not enough of her to share.
The face of an angel, slight dimple in the chin,
A perfect little bundle wrapped in perfect, flawless skin.
Pink rosebud lips, a cute little pout,
Crying for attention and a smile to knock you out.
You know she understands you by the look that's in her eyes,
A unique little miracle full of wonder and surprise.
When she wants attention, she will let you know,
But once you start to cuddle her it's hard to let her go.
So cute and so innocent, a beauty to behold,
All these things and more, and only eight weeks old.
She radiates and sparkles like the stars from up above,
If I had one word to describe her, the word I'd use is 'love'.
She hasn't been here long, she has something that is rare,
It is a kind of wisdom. The who? The why? The where?
If I lived forever I could never express
Feelings that I feel. Joy, pride and happiness.
Well now you know my feelings, there's one last thing to say,
In case you were wondering, it's my baby granddaughter Anais.

Karyl

For Ryan

Ryan you can't disguise the laughter in your eyes.
Ryan, when we hold your hand we understand why we love you.
Ryan when I see you sleeping you look so like her,
Star-sapphire eyes like summer skies gave me this gift so rare.
Ryan maybe one day you will find yourself alone,
May the stars keep watch and guardian angels safely guide you home.
Ryan I love your mother, my lover, my friend,
Three hearts forged together until our worlds end.
Ryan our union is strong, loyal and true and if there is a God,
Then he blessed us with you.
And sometimes we notice a look from the past,
Was it Grandmother's smile or Grandad's laugh?
They watch over you like family do,
Not only on Earth but in Heaven too.
Ryan is for love and Ryan means 'red'
And for all those loved ones now gone ahead,
And for beautiful things we know you will send,
You are our love, our life and our friend.

Andrea Selina Bennett

Different Daffodils

Daffodils in the moonlight,
I had not noticed them before,
How proud they stood in that spring night,
Those daffodils next door.

The slight breeze softly stirred them,
Their heads all nodded away,
It was a chorus of agreement
From that stately floral display.

They looked so pale and ethereal
In the glow of the moon that night,
Not closed up like other flowers
But awake to the silver light.

I saw them from my window,
Those daffodils next door.
They have faded, died and gone now,
But the memory lives evermore.

Shirley R Thomas

WINTER MAGIC

Let the sun shine bright
on a December wedding day,
chase even the darkest
clouds away;
Hear glad voices sing
promises of eternal spring
whatever the changes
our lives may ring;
Like a faerie tide
at the rise of a wintry moon,
may love's starry waves
two hearts entwine;
Feel the magic work for you
that only togetherness brings,
will see us through all
manner of things;
May faith in one another
transcending all belief,
bless twin journeys
through life

R N Taber

Heaven-Sent Helps

Honesty shines through tongues of fire,
Immortal truth alone shall reign.
It lights all minds with fine desire,
Stirs to freedom, life's campaign.

Equity inspires, fills each heart,
With healing for our neighbour's pain.
Neither time nor place can us part,
When warm faithful friends we remain.

Loyalty, the bond of goodwill,
Unites us, though distant, in love.
In one blest communion fulfil,
Glorious in Heaven above.

Purity of thought, wisdom's guide;
Despair gone in bright radiance.
From greed's dark maze we turn aside,
Reaching goodness through providence.

Sincerity free from pretence,
Abhors falsehood and boasted pride.
Spirit of liberty immense,
Crowning honour in us abide.

Heaven-sent ardour indwelling,
Kindles shortcomings with power.
Guides weak steps with strength compelling,
Grants kind helps, the Spirit's shower.

James Leonard Clough

Goodbye Brother

Please don't be sad,
but try to be glad.
All the years you spent together,
remember to good times, not the bad.
Do not feel down,
he would not have wanted you to frown.
Such a big loss is oh, so sad,
and seems oh, so bad.
Even though it is hard
to say goodbye to someone so close to your heart.
Out of sight is all he will be,
as he will always be there with thee.
More so now than ever before,
probably every time to open the door.
He will be so close to you in so many ways,
Maybe not by sight, but always in the light.
So when a quiet moment does appear,
think of him as he will be near,
to share your laughter,
and your pain,
in the sun
and in the rain.
He is your brother and will always be so,
never feel the need to ever let go.
He will always be with you,
returning your love,
the only difference now, it is from up above.

Jennifer Park

Borrowed For This Time

What a bundle of joy, so fresh, so pure,
You make everything in life so secure,
Weak as you are, you bring great strength to me . . .
Entry to my heart, you're holding the key.

I have not borne you, but you are still mine,
Borrowed for this day, and time upon time . . .
Pictures of innocence, unique, complete.
Seeing you grow more this my special treat.

Bringing hope these days as the sun's sure rays . . .
Pure love for you to be bestowed in all ways.
Your hair though wispy, to me burnished gold
Precious moments to grasp and to behold.

Clutching you closely, my heart starts to leap,
When you are at rest, then your bright eyes peep.
You nestle in my arms, free from all care . . .
I tend and feed you, all God's wisdom share.

Each smile and gurgle, this my true reward.
Hidden signs, beauty, to be richly stored . . .
Counting tiny fingers and tiny toes
Love for you grows and grows, soon overflows.

Lesley J Worrall

Marry Me

I tried to find a card to send from me to you
Something not too soppy, sad or blue
A verse that is fun and light-hearted
With something nice to say to you.

Like, you are lovely and very special,
That I enjoy your company,
To say that I love and want you
And will you marry me?

Sally-Ann Hayes

Now, Years On

Now, years on . . .
The mention of his name
Still makes her blood rush
Enough for her to stop still
Swoon and blush!

Nineteenth of March 2001, ringed in red
Only the memory of it lives
Now, years on . . .
When Claire with a friend
Met and spoke to him
Her less than secret dream wish
Her idol . . . and such a dish.

'Sami Hyppia'
Liverpool and Finland football star.

On seeing her crying
He asked, 'What is wrong?'
Claire replied, 'I love you.'

Laughing, he signed her calendar.
Now, years on . . . though out of date
Its occasion, a happy moment to celebrate.

Malcolm Peter Mansfield

GRANDAD'S TEA

As I see the blue of the sky
and the green of the grass,
I think of you.
Things created with beauty in mind,
so I just let my mind, think of you.
Your love in creation,
the birds of the air, sun on the roses
as they glisten with dew -
and I think of you.
It's Grandad's birthday, the children
laugh with glee as they sit in the
garden, around the table -
all to have tea.
There are burgers and Coke - then
ice cream and cake, with candles
lit to blow out - for you and me,
as we sit in the garden to have tea.
And I just let my mind think of you –
Your love in creation - at Grandad's tea -
is God's love for me.

Val Backs

JUST LIKE DADDY

Little man, you're the image of him
who begat you and christened you Jim:
bloated, self-satisfied,
overweight and cross-eyed,
full of wind and incredibly dim.

Norman Bissett

YOUR BIRTHDAY

Your birthday matters.
Its intention –
deeper than convention.
It's a celebration,
a triumph,
of a life -
your life
the gift you have,
the gift you give
to those who love
each day you live.
Your birthday
is like Christmas Day
in a wonderfully personal way -
Your Birth today.

Rosalia Campbell Orr

A HAPPY, HAPPY BIRTHDAY

This to be a first
And a happy one,
Although laid in the garden
About to have fun,
For eye just clocked my cake
With my baby blues
Mum all smartened out
Wearing new shoes,
Yes she looks a picture
Does my nice young mum,
I am hot and sweaty
From laying in the sun.

M D Bedford

THE GATE-LEG TABLE

The woodman's axe had dealt the final blow.
With agonising moan, in motion slow,
The mighty oak began to lean, before
It gathered speed and crashed to forest floor.
Its arms, once proudly reaching for the sky,
Now lay in broken, tangled mass - to die.

But no! Its metamorphosis had begun;
In other forms and shapes had many years to run.
A team of Shires will haul the trunk away
To sawyer's yard to live another day
As timbers for Lord Nelson's ships, maybe
The *Victory* itself - and then to sea.

Less noble fate awaited more maturing
Well-seasoned oak, yet even more enduring.
A carpenter had cast a well-trained eye
O'er stack of oaken planks piled close and high.
He'd been requested by the local squire
To make a gate-leg table, to acquire
As wedding gift for favoured tenant farmer,
To please the young man's future wife, and charm her!

He chose the best of faultless, clear-grained wood
To satisfy his pride and make it good.
He rounded table-top and turned thc legs,
Assembling all with joints and glue and pegs.
No screws were used except to hinge the leaves.
He added slender drawer in under sleeves.

Thus it began its long and useful age;
In farmhouse family room took centre stage.
It's witnessed countless happy, friendly meals,
Excited birthday children's joyful squeals!

And must have heard, of many generations,
Confessions of misdeeds and aberrations,
As who incurred of farmer's wife the ire
By placing steaming pot straight from the fire
On table top, to leave for posterity
Scorch-mark, which defying man's dexterity
Remains. We know, we've tried, it's so ingrained.

It seems the table's come full circle, gained
By us as wedding gift in distant past.
Now ringed with cushioned wheelback chairs, 'twill last
For years to come. Still sturdy legs and frame
And sheen of highly-polished top proclaim
The quality of wood and craft of yore.
As 'table d'hôte' (its literal sense explore!)
It's greeted guests and welcomed with good cheer
Both on and round its board. We hope from here
'Twill long continue in this role, 'til fust
Of time reduces it, like us, to dust.

Geoffrey Matthews

WITH DEEPEST SYMPATHY

Even in the darkness there is a light
Ne'er to be extinguished or grow dim
Shining sure and constant, ever bright,
Such is the greatest love that flows from Him.
So if when night comes round your mind is weary
Or if through the day your heart is aching sore
Just feel His gentle hand upon your shoulder
For He yearns to be your comfort . . . evermore.

Blanche Helena Hall

The Angels Sing

Here beyond the landing,
On the sunny second floor,
In huddled groups a-standing,
Smiling angels guard the door.

There the quiet nursery,
The sun in all its pride
Warms the room so merrily:
The infant sleeps inside.

She dreams of stars and magic;
Of the hope that life can bring;
Unknown times, none tragic.
She just hears the angels sing.

Her life may span so many years,
The angels in their tune
Will not foretell the joy and tears,
This sunny afternoon.

The bird upon the window sill,
Her fledglings in the nest,
Sings her song in murmured trill,
The infant smiles in rest.

For all the world is kind and good,
And none can ask for more.
All things starting as they should.
The angels guard the door.

J A Brown

My Valentine

I know you so completely,
I love you with all my heart,
I feel our souls are fused as one -
That we will never part.

The love we share together,
Increases over time,
Always stay this close to me
And be my Valentine.

Tracey Lynn Birchall

My Friend

His sudden death knocked us all for six,
So full of life and fun, larger than life was he,
It makes you realise, just how brittle life can be.
There one minute, gone the next.
So much unsaid, so much unknown about the real Danny,
Such a massive hole left, with so many stunned and lost,
We gathered at his home with his family,
We all cried and we all laughed as was his way.
At his funeral, it fell to me to say a few words,
To find the perspective, this awful grief to allay,
'Danny and I go back to our boyhood,
He was quite special then, as he is now,
All of you good people here and all those outside,
Knew Danny personally and every one of you I'm sure
Would bear witness,
That he brought to you a smile, a charm, a calm.
He was your best friend, he eased your load,
With our grief, we should also celebrate his life.
I feel he is near us now in our pain.
How many times when things in your life were dire,
Would he arrive with a joke, a twinkle and relight your fire?
We are born into this world only with hope by our side,
Some of us leave unfulfilled, without ruffling any feathers,
A few, like Danny, leave having affected the lives
Of those around him for the better.
Good on you, Danny boy.'

P J Littlefield

The Wedding

We were invited to a wedding at Newcastle Upon Tyne,
We set out rather early and the weather it was fine.
They sent directions where to go, but oh dearie me,
It said turn right at the roundabout, but found at least twenty-three.

Of course we got completely lost, and then a church I saw,
My hat blew off on entering, right out the blinking door.
The bridegroom's mother then walked in and she looked so divine,
When in walked the bride's mother, in a dress the same design.

The bride walked in on Father's arm, so beautiful and fair,
We thought now things have settled, they make a lovely pair.
But no; on taking all her vows, the bride she fainted twice,
They brought a glass of water, Martin said, 'Whiskey would be nice.'

But this saga was not finished, to the reception we had to go,
This was twenty miles away, the rest you surely know.
Yes, we just got lost again, arriving one hour late,
They all gave a slow handclap as we came through the gate.

Ivy Griffiths

Father

F or every time he picks me up when I fall,
A ll of the many times he has,
T wo hands, one big, one small,
H olding as we walked, as we did so many times,
E ven though I'm not your own,
R egardless of that, thank you for loving me, sweet dad of mine.

Cerri Bunce

IN THE DEPTH OF EACH OTHER'S EYES

Come, my love, marry me.
Share with me my dreams.
Shine with me amongst the stars,
Let's race; a comet's tail chase
Across the fiery face of the sun.
Let's celebrate the feast days of December
And frolic under the hot summer days of June.
Let's pack our bags
For a package tour to Mars,
Or how about slowly climbing
The great cratered mountains of the moon?
Shall we bathe in the Sea of Tranquillity?
For lunacy they say, is a great place to be.
With green cheese their savoury speciality.
Or like two valiant Elizabethan galleons
Let's sail the oceans wide,
To drift to the doldrums,
Or sail into some romantic harbour
On the purple dust of the evening tide.
The doors to the different dimensions
Are now thrown open wide,
Let's explore enchanted realms
On white, feathered wings glide
Amongst the capricious clouds,
Under distant alien skies.
But most of all lover, you and I,
Let's discover the land which lies
In the depths of each other's eyes.

Jonathan Pegg

Childish Things

Like the mountain base 'neath the tide's rough kiss
So we, slavish to Time's vile chiding, fade.
Yet, in dogged style, two as one resist
And rouse them to defy the mournful shade.
Slumbering into shape, a dream mistimed
Grows daily, the while we daily decrease,
Confounding the active regime of Time,
Fortifying us against cruel decease.
Beguiling the mind with shapely guesses,
Sweet love structured in the fairest of form,
As proof against Time's wasteful caresses,
The tender heir of Love's invention is born.
Renewing man's lease and thwarting Time's strife,
Ransoming tears, spiting death with a life.

John Dickie

With Best Wishes For . . .

Oh the responsibility of words we owe,
Though working with them in verse and story form,
Away from poetic licence and fictional tale,
The courage vanishes,
Good intentions fail,
Nervous when reality confronts,
Embarrassed too,
True sentiment can, heartfelt, make one a fool,
To write words deeply moving the soul years,
Better just to say,
Many happy returns.

Kathleen Mary Scatchard

11+, Don't Worry Lee

As I look above the fire, a picture is in its place,
A familiar looking portrait, my son, it is his face.
He's growing up so quickly, I don't really take the time
In asking him how he's feeling, after all he's one of mine.

His first day at school only seems like yesterday,
Now he takes his first exam, I'm with him all the way.
I will always stand beside him, make everything fine,
I must encourage and help him, after all, I have the time.

I never had the help when I was his age.
Like turning over a new leaf, we can turn a new page,
I must be there to give him a hand in everything he needs,
Growing up together we can do so many deeds.

He must know not to panic or worry in any way,
With hard work and a good attitude he will make it pay.
So sleep well tonight Son and get plenty of rest,
Because when tomorrow comes, I know you'll do your best.

Geoffrey Graham

Congratulations On The Birth Of Your Baby Boy

We are pleased to know your bundle of joy
Has arrived in the shape of a baby boy.
We hope Mum, Dad and Baby will be happy,
How many times will you change a nappy?
Now Baby is here with a fragrant pong,
Will you sing a lullaby all night long?

Rosemary Davies

BIRTHDAY GREETINGS

He's as daft as a brush,
But a man you can trust:
He's decent, he's honest, upright.
He's known as a treasure
So, just for good measure,
We'll bury him well out of sight.

He's potty, he's barmy,
He's been in the army
And served HRH overseas.
In the Radfan and Aden
He gained decorations
Like OAK and NBG.

He's mad as a hatter,
But that doesn't matter,
On him you may always depend.
Birthday wishes I send
To 'The Colonel', my friend,
Before he goes right round the bend.

Brian M Wood

WARM WISHES

Wishes warm, with love are sent,
for health and wealth and cheeriness,
for blessedness that's heaven-sent,
to fill your day with cheerfulness.

May peace, respect and dignity
combine with memories dear,
may goodwill and tranquillity
envelop those you hold most dear.

This birthday time, may angels guide
and lead you safely confident,
with friendships true, now multiplied,
towards horizons radiant.

Lorna Troop

My First Flight

My mind returned to years gone by
When my friend and I took a sailing trip
To Guernsey for a fortnight's holiday.

The second week we decided
To visit Alderney by plane,
To us this was a real adventure
And really made our day.

We made our way to the airport
And saw this little plane.
(I think Aurigney was its name)
It only took seven passengers,
Each one had to be weighed.

We were at the end of the queue,
But much to our surprise,
We were seated behind the pilot
And had a lovely view.

We still wonder if
It could have left the ground,
With two big ladies in its tail?
How could anyone expect it to fly?

Laura Harris

HAS BEGUN

To each our own, that has in moment
A reason for compare,
In essence glance, a strong enhance,
The moment's come to share,
Share in laughter, call within,
A ring of high proclaim,
It's for those precious moments cared
That we have cause, begin,
In fear not, trend, the day has shown
To each and every word
An oft observe, comes strong accord,
As sense of what is known
Shown in ever sense of time,
Is lustred in its way,
Through it all and understand
As life becomes bouquet
In every sense of wonder why
Have I but gone thus far,
For sole, alone, it has but grown,
Oft 'neath the heavenly star,
Can I but question, part in trend
That has begun of, near
To ever hold, oft to extend
As has before, come clear
Will it be for one and all
To have been known throughout,
There in the keeping, is very well of,
In its coming, is well too, about.

Hugh Campbell

A Holy Land Tour

Gathering His pilgrims
From here and there,
The Lord knew whom to choose.

He must have smiled
As the Boeing soared high,
At the purpose He had for each of us

As we trod in your steps, Lord,
Slowly transformed and fused
Into Your word, seeking the truth.

Our masks began to fall,
Agape loved showed through,
Revealing our need for the touch divine.

Entwined with spiritual truths,
The agony of a nation implanted
In our hearts the seeds of compassion.

Identified with your sacrifice,
We saw the heart of Israel
Pumping its life blood for peace.

You met us in our need,
For me, the baptism of the Spirit
And the gift of tongues
On my birthday!

Alleluia!

Jean McPherson

For Barry

How can I put it into words
For words cannot convey
Just how much you mean to me
How many times each day
I think of you, say thanks for you
And though we're far apart
For you there is a corner
Always in my heart
I have always loved you
From the day that you were born
And I will always love you
Until I too am gone
On this day, your birthday
I will say it loud and clear
I am very proud of you my son
And I love you very much, my dear.

Lydia Barnett

Untitled

Today it is your birthday and I would like to say
Just how much I think of you in my special way
You give so much happiness to everyone you see
Your kindness and thoughtfulness have meant so much to me
When I first met you, I knew from the start
That you were a person who had a special heart
A heart of gold for all the world to know
That is why your family and friends all love you so
So now I would like to make a wish that all your dreams come true
Good luck, good health and happiness be always close to you.

Enid Skelton

CLARE

My beautiful baby just been born,
I was just eighteen,
No one could match what I had,
Lying in my arms in the early morn,
You were so perfect I counted your toes,
I knew then I would never be alone.
So young myself without a thing,
Put her up for adoption, many girls did,
But this was instant love only God could grant,
It was too precious to be real,
What more could I ever want?
They kept you away from me
In a nursery down a long corridor,
Yet I knew your cry among all the rest,
And I came to pick you up, my dear,
For only I knew what you were crying for,
For your mam, I held you tight,
No one could separate us, only the Lord,
I knew He would never do that
Because you were my life,
So we struggled and fought,
We took each day as it came,
No new clothes, no money to be had,
No single parent allowance, not for me.
We were poor and went without,
Those trials and tribulations have long passed,
It was worth the heartache and the strife,
But who cares, we weathered the storm,
Because I've got the most beautiful daughter
That has ever been born.

Kathryn Evans

AUTUMN TO AUTUMN

Pruned roses, gardeners congregating as darkness falls,
Beside water flowing into ornamental pond,
And the last of the summer visitors wend their way
Through rose garden, passing bowling greens and tennis courts,
Into open parkland and darkness.

Christmas shoppers bargain-hunting in twisting lanes,
Pavilion domes showing Brighton's charm in coloured lights,
Carols sung in Steine where Prinny walked, and
Regency houses framed against a winter's sky,
In expectancy of Christmas festival.

Flaying seas, throwing stones on beach now void of deckchairs,
Pier not so busy, waiting for the spring,
Cold winds and salt, sea air, crying seagulls
Mingled with the sound of church bells,
And a boat heading for Shoreham.

Clicking wooden shuttles as fish nets mended,
Sliding brushes as small craft painted.
Coaches, funny hats and candyfloss,
Foreign tongues, mixed dialects,
And boarding houses bursting at the seams.

Blue skies, heat, scantily dressed figures,
Crowded trains, overspilling at railway station,
Music cascading from children's playground,
Photographers taking instant pictures
And Granny in wheeled chair being pushed towards Hove.

Suntanned bodies, mahogany brown,
Mums watching toddlers in paddling pool.
Residents sipping ice-cold drinks on hotel verandahs.
Boats entering and leaving Marina
And the sound of the sea on the pebbles.

Then, as if by magic, landscape changes,
Tints take pride of place
And we peruse once-scented garden,
Hand feeding squirrels,
Listening to the sound of cooing doves
And waiting for the leaves to fall, and autumn.

E M Pucknell

MELTING LOVE

It's a beautiful day although it's raining.
It's a beautiful day, the sun ain't shining.
It's a wonderful world, no one's complaining.
Last night you came home, so I'm not alone.

It's just a beautiful day, although it's snowing.
The sun ain't gonna shine, a cold day forever.
It's a miserable world, everyone's complaining.
Melting love, like melting snow.

Misery, I'm in misery
Since you left and I'm all alone.
My heart is broken now you've gone.
My middle name is Misery.

Your love won't keep me warm,
Tears are still falling, frozen like driven snow.
My heart is slowly breaking,
Melting love, like melting snow.

Now you're back it's a beautiful day.
It's a beautiful day, the sun is shining.
It's a wonderful world, my heart is mending.
Last night you came home, so I'm not alone.

It's a beautiful day; it's a beautiful day.

Ian W Robinson

CHILD OF MY CHILD

(For my grandson, Quinn)

Quinn Robert David, fine manly names
Befitting the child of my child
Who checked into this world in 2002.
You have a special place in my heart,
The space reserved for my first grandchild.
I will follow with affection and interest
Your path to manhood and maturity.
Life's great adventure will be stimulating,
Full of love, laughter, tumbles and tears.
I wish you good health, a questioning mind,
Wisdom and an intuitive perception.
Above all, Quinn, I wish you joy and happiness.

Rose-Mary Gower

ODE TO A LOST LOVED ONE

Sleep sweetly my darling,
Let your dreams reach out to me
Through the depth of the night
And I'll come to you
To caress you as of old.
Whisper my name
And once more my lips
Will tenderly kiss yours.
Our fingers will lovingly entwine
And we shall be as one
Together for all eternity.

S J Roberts

Loadsamoney Course

We are the bright sparks
Team Enterprise gang
Making money and learning
Selling things with a bang

£10 in shares in the company
I have invested free
Christmas boxes, Valentine flowers
Easter chicks sold with a *whee*

I can't wait till this course ends
When I get my money back
Plus a few pounds extra
But come September I'll be back!

H G Griffiths

Birthday Verse

Happy birthday my dear friend
Let friendship never end,
Let's hope there will be many more,
You cheer up my life,
Make little of strife
And of one thing you can be sure,
While you can smile
And put on such style,
Your birthdays get better and better,
Have a great day.

M Rivers

So Special

Oh! What a thrill it gives
That a part of me lives
In someone as special as you.
I hope and pray that you find
When I'm on your mind,
You'll think that
I'm special too.

The joy that abounds
When you are around,
My treasures in life
I can see.
To know you are near,
To feel that you care,
Makes my dearest wish
A reality.

Madge Goodman

Family Treasure

Into our lives she brought much pleasure,
Maia Vianna is our family treasure,
Born in August two thousand and two,
She seems to know what is what, and who is who.
Sister Holly was thrilled on the day
That this little bundle came to stay,
We pray her life be full of fun,
Free from harm and strife,
May the good Lord guide and nurture her,
As she makes her way through life.

Tom Grocott

Baby Worship

A few days after Christmas, early one morn
the first grandchild into my family was born.
'It's a girl, it's a girl,' my daughter shouted with glee
she's beautiful, so pretty, oh do come and see.
Her hair is so auburn and her eyes are so blue,
my heart lifted with joy, she was perfect it's true.
As she has grown, I have witnessed it all:
her first tooth, her first words, even the first time she crawled.
My little granddaughter, so much joy she does bring,
she can wind me round her finger, just like a piece of string.
Such good company, sometimes we visit the zoo,
or climbing frames and slides, the things she makes me do.
Happy and content, and so kind for one so small,
when I get a hug I feel, oh ten feet tall.
She now has a baby brother, who we all worship and adore,
life for me as a nanny, I couldn't wish for anything more.

Shirley Travis

21st Birthday

Birthday greetings
are being sent your way
to wish you happiness
on your big day.
You've reached the age of twenty-one
now isn't that just fun?
Now that you are of legal age
you can do as you desire.
But whatever you decide to do
enjoy your special day.

Linda Casey

Tribute To Someone Special

At our first meeting
two hearts beating,
not in sync.
Tick-tock, tick-tock,
Tick-tock, tick-tock.

Love advanced
quite by chance,
unrecognised.
Tick-tock, tick-tock,
Tock-tick, tock-tick.

Love of deep content,
passion not yet spent.
Satisfied.
Tock-tick, tock-tick,
Tock-tick, tock-tick.

Loyal friend,
companion of my life.
Helen - my wife.
Tick-tick, tick-tick,
Tick-tick, tick-tick.

Robert Allen

To Have And To Hold

I gazed upon her tiny form,
That special day when she was born.
I watched her gently lying there,
Entrusted to my love, my care.

I've watched her grow throughout the years,
We've shared the laughter, shared the tears.
Oh, how those years have swiftly flown,
And how that tiny form has grown.

I've gazed on that same form today,
Resplendent in her bride's array.
What treasured memories I hold,
As snapshots of her life unfold.

My time has come to step aside,
Her bridegroom now does have his bride.
I have, for him, but just one plea,
As I have loved, love her for me.

Sue Lowe

THE DAY I WILL CELEBRATE

The day I will celebrate
Is when God strikes those
Evil ones down.
I will jump for joy,
Shout from the rooftops,
'Those evil b******s are
No longer around.
God has kicked them to the ground.'
My heart smiled, has God
Kicked them so hard
They are never to be found?
My soul laughs.
Even Hell will not let them be redeemed.
Oh what cowards they are,
Listen to them cry and scream.
My time has come
To truly celebrate.
When God wiped that scum out
From underneath my face.

Jenifer Ellen Austin

CELEBRATIONS IN VERSE

Celebrations in verse
Can mean a wedding, anniversary or birth
For some is well their worth
And others are just a curse

Celebrations in verse
Are celebrated all year long
And in no time they're gone
When you're growing up they come and go
For when you're older you don't want anymore

Celebrations in verse start with the first month of the year
And for the rest you will get a big cheer
Others believe in reading their horoscope
Where some will sit and take dope

Celebrations in verse
Start with Aries and end with Pisces
But there are more than these
Besides Leo, Virgo, Libra and Capricorn
Plus the rest that are well known

Celebrations in verse
Gemini and Libra are just two signs that match
As well as Taurus and Virgo who are also a good catch.

Coleen Bradshaw

RAINBOW'S END

At the end of a rainbow there is a pot of gold,
So goes the story we've always been told.
Legends so ancient and stories so old -
I've found my rainbow with a pot of gold.

My friend is my rainbow, her heart is of gold,
Just look and you'll find what cannot be sold.
Just reach out and touch, just be so bold
And you too can find somewhere such a heart of gold.

Helga Dharmpaul

My Marriage

In 1984 on the morning of March the third,
The ringing alarm clock I heard.
Joyfully I stepped out of bed,
It was the morning I was to be wed.
To the church I briskly walked
Alongside my brother, who constantly talked.
I stood outside and the sun shone down,
As time passed, my brother began to frown.
'You'd better go inside,' he said, above the street's din.
'I'm going for a walk,' I replied, scratching my chin.
While walking, I wondered would our big day falter,
Maybe I would be left alone at the altar.
Returning to the church, I greeted family and friends,
And entered, waiting for my single life to end.
My earlier fears were not justified,
Music played and Mandy appeared before my eyes.
As she reached me, I gave a broad smile,
The priest read the vows which we then repeated,
While all our guests remained seated.
When he announced, 'You're now man and wife,'
Cameras clicked and people gave goodwill messages
For the rest of our life.
I was happier than ever before,
Marrying Mandy was the best thing I've ever done,
That's for sure.

Graeme Doherty

The Day I Knew I Loved You

It was a very strange day
Because of what I'd say
On the day I knew I loved you.

It wasn't really planned
That I would reveal my hand
And tell you that I loved you.

But those words that I'd said
Bounced around in my head
Once I'd told you that I loved you.

And all day I was in a daze
My mind filled with haze
Because I'd said I loved you.

Even next day on the way to work
Written in the dust and dirt
On the car in front, 'I love you.'

But those words were so true
When I'd said them to you
Because I loved you, and still do.

Carl Gravestock

Mother

When I was a baby you nursed me
And gave me strength and health.
It must have been a struggle
For we did not have great wealth.

As I grew up you were always there
When I needed your advice.
I didn't always take it
For the young are so unwise.

Now I'm getting older
I don't know how to thank
You, who are so good to me,
I've no money in the bank

To shower you with gifts,
And so I'll simply say,
Oh Mother, may God bless you,
On this and every day.

Joyce Walker

WEDDING BELLS

All is peaceful now, as I sit alone
The children have gone, the birds have flown;
This was a very special day
Today I gave my daughter away.

The church was 'decked and at every pew
Hung garlands and ribbons: pink, green and blue;
Flowers adorned in their full bloom
Both the church and the bride and groom.

The choir sang those familiar songs
The vicar going on and on;
Until at last it was proclaimed for life
'Let them be husband and wife.'

The sermons stop, the speeches begun
Then there was food and drink for everyone;
Later you could dance, if you felt like that
Or just sit together, laugh and chat.

Then finally a boot, a tin
Tied to the car they will be in;
Then off they go, the bride and groom
To enjoy their honeymoon.

Georgina Slape

THE THIRD GRANDCHILD

Another life is growing,
The third grandchild.
This baby will be special,
A milestone
Our children have put in place.
Now all three have been replaced.
Inside ourselves we scamper like lambs,
But they will see us as old,
Eventually in faded photographs
Edged with muted gold.
But before that happens
We have time and love,
Passions to pass on
From the world above
The cradle.
Passions for what every day brings.
Gifts for this new little baby,
Of poems and stories and beautiful things.

Pat Morton

HAPPY BIRTHDAY

This time of the year
Comes only but once,
Live life to the full,
Do not ever let it be dull.

Another year older,
Older brain cells,
More and more wrinkles,
Which set off alarm bells.

Think of the positives
And not of the negatives,
And do not let any bad thoughts get in the way
Of you enjoying your birthday.

Shauneen Malone

To My Daughter On Her Eighteenth Birthday

On this day of all days
I can't help but view the past,
From the moment you could toddle
The years have gone so fast.
I've stood by many milestones
And cheered you going by,
And now and then I've pushed you
On the steep and narrow way.
I always knew you'd make it
For your heart is strong and true,
And whatever life may hand you,
You've the strength to carry through.
The path that you must travel
Is a path much trod before,
Parts of it are wonderful
While others leave you sore;
But I'll be on the sidelines
To encourage and console,
And my prayers are always with you
As you reach and pass each goal.
Whatever life my bring you,
All I wish is happiness
And love and true fulfilment,
May your road through life be blessed.

Caroline Isherwood

PAX CAKES ON PALM SUNDAY

Spring once more beside the flowing river,
A tiny church where folk stand in a ring.
Village school with children in a quiver,
Hold lowly donkey bearing Christ the King.

Palm Sunday donkey standing by the porch door,
Excited children run to meet their King,
Carefully placing fronds across the church floor,
With scented heather twigs and fragrant ling.

Ride on, ride on, in majesty they cry,
The choir sing out with clarity and verve,
While smiling actors dressed as passers-by
Call out hosanna to the king they serve.

Bread and wine are blessed beside the altar,
The wafer and the cup are held aloft,
And on this day with psalm from ancient Psalter,
Responses made and holy wine is quaffed.

Service over, benediction spoken,
A special token now is given out,
A pax cake to each worshipper is given,
Good neighbour and true peace, the children shout.

Norma B Rudge

FOR MY DAUGHTER

Joy touches my hand when I'm sleeping
Comforts and a single act of celebration absorb me.
Resting in a scarlet slumber
The anatomy of my body becomes a monochrome photograph
Of my daughter's beautiful face.
Warmth and solitude; I love you.

Ethan Madison

Untitled

Do you, my friend, reaching eighty-five,
recall our country garden tryst?
We neither of us could resist
Amethyst and peach that still survive,
A mesmeric, subtle thought motif
I trust embellishes your day;
arborial frieze in jade relief -
does this, ensconced in blessing stay?
Such instances, few and far between,
we shared, live on in memory:
savour in your soul what bliss has been,
pin hope in astral galaxy.
Through racing aeons exaltation flees
but now, upon your day of birth,
the law of averages decrees
your due of dreams come true on Earth.

Ruth Daviat

Above Sin

Why do
I know
That I
Am happy
Above all?
I am
Above the
Fall I
Am not
Entitled
To.

Nicola Barnes

Dedication Day

Sweet little treasure, gift from above,
Bringing to us such pleasure and love.
Today is so special and this is our prayer,
The Lord guard and keep you in His tender care.
And for your parents, we earnestly pray,
As they seek to guide and teach you His way,
That His love and blessing will rest on you all
And early in life may you answer the call,
To follow the Shepherd, keep close to His side,
Knowing Him as your Saviour, your true friend and guide.
Into His hands we commit you today,
For He is the life, the truth and the way.
May the faith of your parents become your faith too.
This is the prayer we are praying for you.
Sweet little treasure, dear baby boy,
Thank you for filling our hearts with such joy.
Lovingly now, your grandparents say,
Every blessing on this dedication today.

Eileen Phillis

Dad

You did reach the millennium plus a year, then two,
And I will not forget the love that I received from you.
You fooled them all, my special dad, till God knocked on the door,
'Come home my son, you've had your life, can't give you anymore.'

Yet life goes on, you always said, this I know is true,
And I don't need a special day just to remember you.
So as you look from Heaven and watch me soldier on,
Don't think that I've forgotten and the memories have gone.

I think about you all the time, my childhood could not be,
If you had not been in my life to care and cherish me.
So when you see me laughing, or days when I look sad,
It's because I loved you dearly and I miss my dear old dad.

K Townsley

NOVEMBER BABY

Of all the babies I have had and held,
There's none to compare to Kurtis, my grandson,
So perfect in his mould.
Bright blue eyes, the mirror of his mother,
Chubby cheeks and tiny double chin
That dimples when he smiles.
He's nearly five months now and really starting to grow.
At first he seemed so small and frail,
Suffering from colic, he suffered so.
Lots of gurgling in his own language,
From breast to bottle putting on the pounds.
His little head crowned with down,
A complexion to be envied,
Long eyelashes resting on tiny cheek bones
In sweet repose.
The sweetest tiny nose and lips like Cupid's bow.
He's dressed in little clothes, so clean and smart
He's win the 'Baby Show.'
I'm biased I know, but he's my first grandchild,
Kurtis, and I love him so.
I dedicate these loving words to my daughter,
Thanking God for these blessings,
That fill my heart with joy.
When she reads this, she will certainly know.

Liz Dicken

Happy Day

A celebration full of glee
Was when my first-born came to be.
Singing, dancing, family joy,
A handsome, full-formed, bouncing boy.
Regard those features carved in love,
Wide open eyes ready to rove.

Regard those grasping fingers: ten.
What to catch? And where and when?
Regard this body, sure and firm
What potential lies within?
A football star, a striker true?
A scholar with a high IQ?

Wherever his own future lay,
He made me oh, so proud that day.
A day which I will always treasure,
I owe him love without measure.

Cyril Joyce

A Ruby Wedding

Forty years of marriage is a Ruby Wedding.
After forty years of marriage, you know where you are heading.
Your family are proud of you two,
With all their love, which is your due.
Sweet moments shared between you both,
With love and goodness for you both.
With family and friends you celebrate
To make this day really great.

Zoe French

My Christmas Gift Was Christopher

On Christmas Day 40 years ago,
Santa didn't come with a yo-ho-ho.
He came with oh, such joy,
Because I was blessed with a beautiful boy.

This child is so loving and caring,
All his love, he just keeps sharing.
Christopher I am so proud of you,
All your love and kindness sees me through,

From deep in my heart I can honestly say,
You have 40 years of love on this, your birthday.
From the day your life began,
I was so proud to be your mum,
But I am even prouder to say,
You are my son.
Happy birthday and happy Christmas,
On your 40th you just stand tall,
Because you're the greatest gift of all.

Rosalind Jennings

Twenty-One Today

A message to the one I love sent on this special day,
With warm congratulations sent in a special way.
Because it is your birthday, the party has begun,
You're not just one year older, today you're twenty-one.
So I send you special wishes, all wrapped in love for you,
To tell you how I need you and to say my love is true.
So have a happy twenty-first, I drink to you a toast,
Of all the gifts you may receive, my love is worth the most.

S Brown

UNTITLED

My son's to be a grandad,
Can this news be true?
Nic and Neil have told us
The test result was blue.

In my day things were secret
'Twixt prospective mums and dads,
Until it was so obvious
There was to be a newborn lad.

But wait, it may not be a boy,
Do I really want to know?
Can I be patient for so long
Or find out what the scan will show?

It's taken several months now
And at last we have been told,
Excitedly we can expect
A baby girl to join the fold.

I'm soon to be a great-grandma,
I repeat the fact aloud,
I'm sure the little sweetheart
Will make me very proud.

Doreen W Harvey

SIAN ELIZABETH

Precious Sian Elizabeth - may God bless you today,
You have a place within my heart where always you will stay,
You are everything to Grandma, tender, soft and sweet,
A darling, dainty, little girl to make my joy complete.

I wish for you so many things to gladly fill your days,
For happiness, good health and love to follow you always.
How proud I am to hold you dear, on this your christening day,
May God's love keep you evermore safe and sound I pray.

Maria Daines

CELEBRATION OF DAD'S LIFE

A sad goodbye to you my friend,
Now you have reached your journey's end.
We all will miss your twinkling eyes,
'Tis time our paths must part.

Yet memories will never fade,
Such love of life as you displayed
Still lingers on, though you have gone,
Embedded in our hearts.

So I shall chase the hops tonight
And raise my glass to you,
To ponder on sweet memories,
As you would wish me to.

Then should I reach grey twilight hours,
Depression dawning fast,
The memories I hold inside
Will help sad moments pass.

Quiet tears that fall from misty eyes,
No sobbing, bleating, gasping sighs,
'Tis silence weeping to your peaceful sleeping,
As I say my last goodbyes.

Love you Dad, Charlie.

C H Baker

HANNAH AND MARK'S WEDDING CELEBRATIONS

In Trinity Mews it was night
and Chucky and Edward, the hamsters,
were playing in the moonlight
for their master and mistress would be celebrating
their marriage on the morrow
and for them that was no sorrow,
but more seed to eat and water to drink,
and for master and mistress
their pens would be wet with ink.

Hannah and Mark are to sign the register
and perhaps they might travel to Leicester,
for Hannah comes from Birmingham and
she loves the Black Country, but both her
and Mark likes Ireland,
to sample the Guinness from the River Liffey
not so silly.
Their reception will be like a West End production,
that night of nights,
where Hannah in her crimson velveteen gown
will capture Mark in his bespoke town.
Hannah and Mark will be happy,
though there will be times when both become a little snappy,
but Chucky and Edward will play and play
for another day,
when Hannah and Mark, their vows exchanged, will love
each other to produce a child.
Boy or girl, it matters little,
happiness will be complete
as these little children grow to be model
siblings of their parents' glow.
God bless you Hannah, God bless you Mark,
you have made a splendid start.

Gerard Allardyce

AND THE LADY CAST A ROSE UPON THE SEA

Father's Day, strolling on the seafront at Penarth,
Outdoor cafes, smiling families.
Ice cream coated children's faces,
Warm summer breezes, gently moving flags.

Distant boats, bobbing like corks, to laughter,
Skimming pebbles from the beach.
Dads spoilt with Sunday lunches,
Mums relaxed, under bright parasols.

Walking back towards the pier
The brass band strains upon the air.
Sitting on a bench of sea-washed boards,
Listening to the music and the sea.

A happy Father's Day, as children danced and sang,
And clapped in time to trumpet, pipe and drum.
Gulls and other sea-bound birds aloft,
Joining in the choral song and dance.

Then she was there, walking to us,
Head held high, yet sad.
Dark glasses, hiding sun and tears,
A fresh-picked flower clasped to her heart.

We turned towards each other, as she passed
Tears filled our eyes, a poignant moment,
As on she walked, to find a quiet place,
And the lady cast a rose upon the sea.

We hoped she thought of bygone, happy days,
And prayed her heart would be at peace.
The band played on, the children sang,
And the lady cast a rose upon the sea.

Glyn Davies

GOLDEN DAYS

On this your Golden Wedding day
I wish you fifty more
Each year to be as happy
As the one before

I'm sure the years have vanished
And you can't think where they've gone
But many more will lie ahead
Starting this day on

The family that you raised have now
A family of their own
By following in your footsteps
Their love has bloomed and grown

There's another generation
That's following up behind
That will follow your example
To be loving and to be kind

Not only to each other
But to all along the way
With respect for other's feelings
Every single day

But this day is just for the two of you
A celebration of who you are
It's a thank you for just being there
And the life you've shared so far.

Jackie Johnson

WITH ALL MY HEART

I've gone on before you
But have to make clear,
My love is still with you
Although I'm not here.

I made some mistakes,
The same as the rest.
If you love me, you'll know
That I did do my best.

I loved you, in life,
For just being you.
That won't ever alter,
Whatever you do.

Don't have guilty feelings,
No sadness, no strife.
Remember me laughing,
Enjoying my life.

Don't grieve that I've gone,
I'll see you again.
I'll be waiting to greet you,
So please, until then . . .

Be the best you can be,
Be loving, be true,
Be there for each other
And know I love *you*.

Anne Gardiner

A Part

Conceived in lust and love and joy,
Spice-sugared girl? Snail-sluggard boy?
Earth waits - but first with me embrace
The same stretched symbiotic space.

Come Nature, wave your wondrous wand,
Great God Incarnate, bless the bond,
For children all, for womankind,
Feed the placenta, feed the mind.

Though sometime weary, sore, unwell,
I will vouchsafe your citadel,
But steel yourself, my child, to hear
Vain manic glee and tragic tear.

Oh kicking brat, oh monstrous girth,
The time has come for bloody birth,
My precious infant, for our sins,
Our life asunder now begins.

Peter Davies

Angels

(In memory of my father)

We are all angels here on Earth
From the mystery of the time of birth
Then when we die
We go to be angels in the sky

When our time has come to die
Our loved ones stand around and cry
They don't want us to go
They're full of bitterness and woe

But the time comes for us all
Our guardian angel comes to call
The pain will get too much to bear
Then we drift without a care

Do not weep for your loved one this way
He will wake to a bright new day
We have to let go and say goodbye
We'll meet - when we're angels in the sky.

Margaret Marston

We Wish Them Well

Seventy years their two hearts entwined
In this passing flight of time,
When they were young, took their vows
Beating as one together now,
Grown together over the years,
Through ups and downs, laughter, tears
Children came to bless their days,
Gently nurtured in loving ways,
Friends, relatives, loved ones come,
Always welcome to their home.
Middle age has much to say,
Children's children come to stay,
'Nan and Grandad play with me,
Mum and Dad are busy as bees.'
Family values stand in stead,
The life that they together lead,
Getting old, there's no such thing,
Like two birds upon the wing.
Great grandchildren come along,
To keep them young in heart and song,
Always together, whatever the weather,
Always still in love with one another.

George Camp

HAPPY BIRTHDAY

Your birthday comes around, once more
To bring you lots of things in store
So many blessings for this day
So much happiness, for this, your birthday

When you open each envelope
Hope you will be able to cope
With each word that brings such gladness
Those loving words that express, such loveliness

When you unwrap your presents, dear
Hoping that it is so very clear
That we think of you so very much
Just return a kiss with thanks, and a gentle touch.

Birthdays come and birthdays go
Although, this day is special so
Although the ripe age of sixty-one
God bless you now, and till the day is done

So, when you take that wish or two
Hope your dreams come true
So, now I wish you a very happy day
With so much cheer, I gladly pray.

Jean P McGovern

WELCOME

Mobile face and kicking legs, tear-washed dimple cheeks,
tiny person, cosy, dependent small creation.
I pick you up to feel new warmth.
Still in some awe at this urgent life,
at once so intimate
but now on daily show!

FAC

YOU WILL KNOW

You have gone to another place
where only your smile and truth are known.
A place where there are no more problems
and you need never be alone.

You will have met all who went before
and know all who are yet to come.
You will have totted up your 'living'
and equalised the sum.

You will have solved the 'Mystery of Life'
and know why you were 'here'.
You will have heard the Heavenly choirs
and not known any fear.

You were 'here' at your end
and 'there' at your start.
You will also know that forever
you'll live on in someone's heart.

Maureen Thomas

ALWAYS BY YOUR SIDE

She is your guardian angel,
A star, bright in the sky,
Looking down at you, so proud.
Resting at peace, so warm,
Her love with you forever,
Keeping you safe in her thoughts.
Memories will be with you always,
A picture of someone you love,
Your mum, may be far away,
But will always be so near.

Helen Walsh

A Celebration Of Spring

Countryside and woodland waken to new life
As spring's verdant buds begin to show;
Hedgerows tremble with vernal expectancy
While flowers unfold and trees blossom again.
Fields and meadows, born anew, begin to sing
Their idyllic lays of pastoral love,
Bursting into buttercups and dancing with daisies;
Oceans of golden yellow on fire
Blend with poppy seas aflame with crimson.

From riots of red to cool sylvan shades,
Where forest floors turn into bluebell carpets
And overhanging boughs come into leaf.
Nature opens wide the gates of spring
As branches, live with sap, break out into bloom;
Diaphanous domes of canopied carpentry,
Garlanded with hammocks of greenery,
Smile upon a labyrinth of fountain springs
Fed by the purest crystal streams.

And now, upon a greensward of deepest emerald,
The first young song thrush of spring alights,
Descanting his three - and four - note refrain,
While from the overarching panoply of leaves
There descends a silver melody of trills and warbles
As songbirds enchain their sweet odes of praise
To their creator. And as robin, wren and song thrush
Join with blackbird, nightingale and lark,
All creation's harmonies sing His glory.

For He alone is Lord of Heaven and Earth,
And His word will live on for evermore.

Robert D Hayward

United The Kingdom

Daffodil, thistle, shamrock and rose
A bouquet of Britain where free-thinking grows
Who march for causes they believe
The wrong to overcome
Remembering history can be changed
By just the voice of one.
Yes, pilgrims onward in this land
Oft choose the harder path
And brace themselves to follow right
Whate'er the aftermath.
Back dialogue and compromise
To chain the hounds of war
Be deaf their ears to subtle spin
That champions blood and gore.
With compassion tend the sick
View asylum with concern
Do not succumb to black road-rage
In all things queue your turn.
Knowing their taste in DIY
Is sometimes not in keeping
And reckless overspending
May end in future weeping.
Believing that pursuit of wealth
Is not life's only fare
Yet chance and buy a ticket
To become a millionaire.
Understanding that some matters
Have their end in sorrow
So citizens stand face-to-sun
Towards a better morrow.

Sarah Blackmore

A JUBILEE, A CELEBRATION

Let's have a party
A huge celebration
Pack 50 years into a weekend
You can use my back garden
Invite a few friends round
Serve strawberries and salmon roulade

Let's have proms at the palace
A pageant of music
A galaxy of fireworks and stars
We'll have Handel, McCartney
Trail beacons, sound fanfares
Jubilation for those golden years

Start with ducks in the park
In waddling formation
Taking the quiet salute
Then a gold coach procession
An dancers in costume
Pomp and ceremony comes easy to us

Let's have a banquet
And toast a few speeches
We'll invite the Lord Mayor around
Colourful flags waving
And cheering street-liners
With thousands of voices in song

We'll light up the palace
And take a few encores
Mega stars reach for the sky
A choreographed fly-past
Is how we shall end it
An extravaganza on high

Val Stephenson

A Birthday Greeting

It is your birthday again,
It comes around so soon.
How's your cake for candles,
Is there plenty of room?
I am not being funny,
I have known you so long,
It sounds like a line
From a very old song.
But, honestly though,
It is a pleasure to send
Loving birthday greetings
To such an old friend.
So fill up your glass,
Have plenty of fun,
With presents galore
And cards by the ton.
I cannot be with you
On this lovely day,
There are many more things
That I could say.
I hope to meet up with you
Again, very soon,
Maybe talk of a holiday,
I'd be over the moon.
Good luck, good health
Go with you always,
God's special blessings
To the end of your days.
A happy birthday to you,
These words I send,
With loving thoughts
To my very old friend.

Joan Smith

How True!

(See Deuteronomy ch18 vss 19 to 22 JB)

Many works are celebrated
Viewed as awe-inspiring,
So how may one distinguish that
Which is true, from God, enduring?

The rules from Him, so long ago
Change not, tho' thousands of years
May come and go, in war, in peace, so
What did He say, helping us through fears?

'Whatever is said, must honour Him, God;
The prophet spoke, let all take note,
Came true, not one word a blot.
But if proved false, a lie this was, not from God he wrote.'

It must come true *and* honour God,
Not back down, nor change a thing.
For false prophets come and these will go,
Not assured protection or, His blessing.

A verse to celebrate and shout:
'Praise be to God, for living!
Thank you, for taking note
Our heart's inner motivating.'

And may you take from those who judge,
Though given no approval,
The elevated stance they take no pledge,
Allow you, God Eternal.

Gerasim

PRECIOUS CHILD

To be blessed with the birth of a child,
Is a blessing to be really treasured,
The love and joy you feel
Is so big it can never be measured.

A child is so very precious,
So cradle and nurture it with care,
Put all material things behind you,
For your child you must always be there.

If you care for the little one properly,
Your child will grow to be big and strong,
Make sure you give it plenty of love and happiness,
So it will know how to pass good values and love on.

To be a perfect parent
Is an impossible task,
Never work for perfection,
As perfection is just a mask.

None of us are perfect,
We all make mistakes along the way,
But taught right from wrong from the beginning,
With plenty of love, your child won't stray.

As a parent your job won't be easy,
With sleepless nights, your temper frays,
Treat your child like a delicate flower,
Give it love and respect always.

Gillian S Gill

Empathy

The chemistry of love is highly complex
It is not entirely bound up with our sex
It can function between bodies of the same kind
And sometimes operate fully entirely in the mind

Sexual empathy is in our animal ancestry
Our genes impel us to the opposite sex
It is nature's way of ensuring our future destiny
But this can take place with a partner who can vex

True empathy however is something God-like
It transcends anything else we know in living
And we recognise it at once when it decides to strike
For it is when the Lord bestows on us His giving

From then on in our lives we are not alone
We know that there is someone else who cares
No matter if the rest of the world is hard as stone
To our empathy together nought compares

If tragedy intrudes to harm our bliss
It is not the end for our memories will then remain
As we recall every moment from that first kiss
Sustained by a sure reunion to come in God's domain

When I bid my friends and relatives 'God Bless'
It is really this unique empathy I wish for them
I have known of it and can still feel its loving caress
And I know that on this earth nothing finer that it can stem

It is God's greatest gift to us of either gender
But we also have our active, positive part to play
By unselfishly to our fellow human beings our love to render
For then suddenly empathy will assuredly come to us some day

And we will revel with our partner in our new and different life
Guarded now forever by our love against all future human strife.

Frank Hansford-Miller

HOSTAGE TO FORTUNE

Ring out the old year to the sound of adieu, adieu,
the old year's going, it's time to ring in the new.
Champagne and fireworks at the stroke of Big Ben,
brothers in celebration, Grand Hotel to the Wig and Pen.

Bar talk is really frantic, hopes for twenty-zero-three,
dreams and ambitions, we all trust we hold the key.
Whether something to be gained, or something to be lost,
we can be a hostage to fortune, living to pay the cost.

Bar talk is exhausted, and the champagne's run dry,
and those dreams and ambitions can so easily just die.
But we owe it to ourselves, we have a true destiny,
don't be a hostage to fortune, this twenty-zero-three.

Keith Leese

LAURA AND CLARE

Sometimes the nine months seemed to go on forever,
Then I'd feel a movement and the wait is worthwhile,
Not knowing if it was a boy or girl
Added to the excitement.
Apprehension setting in as the date draws near,
No going back now, the waiting nearly over,
Holding my daughters after arriving
Safely into the world,
My husband, Hugh, at my side,
The surge of love,
The joys still to come,
I'm a mother now,
And so very lucky.

Ann Sykes

The Wedding

It was a day sublime and sweet,
When Laura and Jon in church did meet.
In stunning gown, gliding down the aisle,
Walked happy the bride with radiant smile.
Vows were witnessed of lasting devotion,
Expressed heartfelt with deep emotion.
Warm words exchanged by groom and bride,
Raised tears of sentiment none could hide.
Tread not on my dreams, by Yeats on humility,
Was voiced by Gramps with all sincerity.
A reception of perfection continued good feeling,
Enhanced by speeches entertaining, revealing.
Married life may sometimes cause concern,
But fond memories of this day will always return.

Bill Newham

Goodbye To Parents

The pain of parting, yet awhile
Will give you grief I know
But I have had a happy life
Because you loved me so.

Try to remember happier times
Those days a while ago
Not of the careworn mother
But of the girl you used to know.

The faith that you have given me
Will hold me fast, no pain
So God bless you both my darlings
Until we meet again.

M Sanderson

Our World

I love the ocean with its foaming waves
And long, sunny, hazy days,
Sandy beaches and rocks covered in spray,
I can while many hours away.

Watching birds flying oh, so high
And hills that seem to reach the sky
Sitting by a babbling brook,
Pen and paper and a favourite book.

Seeing pine trees, tall and straight
And wild flowers, that round every bend await.
The sunset and the sunrise,
Every day a new surprise.

Perhaps, in time, man will learn to be
Content with the beauty that comes for free
And instead of war and strife
Will understand there is much more in life.

Heather Moore

From Acorns To Oak Trees

From the basic bond of blood-lines - the animated seed
Has rushed amid the flood-lines to nurture and to feed.
A natural propagation secure within its tomb,
Genetic destination provided in the womb.
Then tossed into this big, wide world with kith and kin around,
Like little flags or leaves unfurled - the young will find their ground.
The family will grow with care and blossom at its head.
Then later, so much grief will share, when burying its dead.
So from the simple, tiny spawn - of love and happy mirth,
A vast, dynamic unit forms - the strongest link on Earth.

Pearl M Burdock

24th May 2003

Summer Marie, just look at you now,
It's your birthday, you're one year today.
Looking back, your birth brought worry and fear,
But you knew on this Earth you wanted to stay,
As the days went by, you grew so weak.
You had to fight for the right to live,
Great Ormond Street Hospital was your only hope,
With skilled surgeons, their help and time to give.
Your tiny heart was worked on,
For seven hours everyone prayed.
You made it, all prayers were answered.
What a marvellous recovery you made.
Now you're a gorgeous baby girl,
Delighting in the world you see,
The scars are fading, you're fit and well
Enjoying each day, lively as can be.
Your parents are so proud
Of the beautiful daughter they love.
A blue-eyed smiling miracle
Sent from Heaven above.

J Cooke

It's A Baby Boy

Little hands like starfish
Little angel face,
A beautiful little baby boy
Given by God's grace.

And when he gives his first real smile,
The first milestone is past
But there are many more to come
It will not be the last.

But these are all in the future
For this tiny little mite
May his coming bring great happiness
And each day a new delight.

Isobel Laffin

For Gill . . .

Our day is here, no more waiting, planning or counting,
A day to declare our love for each other, a love that's unsurmounting,
Everyone awaits you, friends, family and most of all me,
But they'll never understand how deep my love can be.

Like a river it runs forever, it's strong, it's sometimes raging,
Nothing can ever stop it, it's timeless, never ageing.
When sun shines on the river I feel your warmth, it goes right through,
When the moon shines on the river, it reflects my eternal love for you.

When you're not here, there is only darkness, I cannot smile, I cannot laugh,
But this river, it runs regardless, for it knows no other path,
It travels over mountains, it cascades from up above,
It winds its way through valleys, until it reaches its bay of love.

You'll never know how much I love you, a love you must uncuff,
So I can wrap my love around you, for words are not enough,
Stay with me, laugh with me, dance with me,
Lay with me, wake with me, romance with me.

My love for you knows no bounds, it's plain for all to see,
It warms you, it surrounds you, from here to eternity.
Come take this river of love, bring it to the bay,
My love I lay before you Gill, on this our wedding day.

M Purcell

When I Die

When I die I shall just slip away to another world.
I will not know what to expect.
I will not know who'll be there.

When I die, I know that you'll be sad.
I know that you'll cry. I expect that.
After a while I beg you to try and live a life
Without my arms, without my voice and be happy.

When I die, I want you to know that
I'm only 'up there'. Nothing's changed.
You can still talk to me. You can still laugh with me.
I shall always listen.

When I die, I'd like you to remember the
Good times, or even bad times.
They are all memories.
Nobody can take them away.

When I die, my biggest wish is to ask you
To try really, really hard to be brave.
I love you and you love me.
That will always be the same.

Lynn Craig

Your Baby's Christening

Today is the beginning
Of your baby's Christian faith,
As vows are made on his behalf
Upon his christening date:
Now his life will surely be
Guided in Christ's ways,
May his pathway see him blessed
Through all his childhood days

And when godparents' tasks are through
And comes his confirmation,
May he make those vows himself
With sure determination,
Then throughout his precious life
He'll know he's blessed to be
Loved in such a special way
By his whole family.

Peter Fordham

Crystal In The Snow

I saw you standing there,
Lonely in your rain.
I felt an empathy,
Of your sadness and pain.
I cried out to comfort you,
Offer a gentle word.
But all of my loving,
Could not always be heard.
I still want to tell you,
I still want you to know.
You are so beautiful,
A crystal in the snow.
A dew ball on the grass,
A raindrop on my window.
I chose you as my friend,
And forever that is so.
Wherever you may wander,
Wherever you may rest.
I will always love you,
You are my very best.

Carol Ann Darling

On Reaching Fifty

Once you reach fifty, you suddenly find
Life throws you that second chance
And all of the women who once passed you by
Have started to give you that glance
You don't need a pep, there's a spring in your step
Life is sunny, you can't help but smile
And all those who will say you're over the hill
Are jealous, you're top of the pile!

Now in a morning you jump out of bed
Take a stretch and feel like a tower
What used to take minutes to wash
Now takes anything up to an hour!
You discard the grey, got to sprinkle and spray
Look your best for what lies ahead
You don't need to work full time anymore
'Cause you're drawing your pension instead!

Today's the day you wait in the hall
Soon your first cheque will come in the post
You've waited so long for this day to come round
To buy the things you've wanted the most
You hear footsteps out on the drive
As your letter is pushed through the door
But then quicker than lightning you're brushed aside
It's whisked away before it reaches the floor.

She says, 'Don't worry dear, I'll see to this, I've a plan which is going to gel,
I've drawn up a short list of things that we need,
Your money'll do ever so well
What's mine is mine
And what's yours is mine
And don't stand there looking so bland
I can see you're feeling a little confused
But don't worry, you'll soon understand!'

And your daughters, your best friends that you always thought
Their ideas they've already lent
There's catalogues and brochures all over the floor
Your first cheque they've already spent
You feel like a carcass picked clean in the sun
Yet the vultures are braying for more
And with nowhere to turn, you put on your coat
And quietly slip through the door

You get out your golf clubs and load up the car
And the wife says, 'Excuse me, my dear
I know my memory's not overly great
But didn't you play sometime last year?
The bedrooms need painting, the handrails are loose
And when I dusted our portrait it fell
You've got all these jobs, it'd be a shame to fall out
Just when we're doing so well.'

Yes, once you reach fifty, you suddenly find
Life's not altered, not one little bit
You still wear the trousers but that's just because
The skirt and the blouse don't fit
You still get blamed for washing left in the rain
And for dishes piled up in the sink
Still there's always the coal house, it's dark and it's damp
But at least there you can have a quiet drink.

Steven Krzymowski

UNTITLED

On that wonderful day you arrived,
Until we met lived, yet not alive,
Each day of my life, simply contrived,
Now spirit and hope have plainly revived,
On that wonderful day you arrived.

Tina Arnold

Hero

What makes a hero? He could be a fire-fighter who saved the child,
She could be the driver who pulled open the car door
When it burst into flames,
It could be the father who took the time to play with his son,
A mum who tells her daughter she is lovely after bring dumped,
A jogger who falls at the finish line,
To get up again in the name of charity,
A hero could pass you in the street and you would never know it.
They could do something so simple it would take your breath away,
Many would risk their lives for you, there are also the quiet ones
Who are always there, you see them all the time
They are the unsung heroes from everyday life,
Every walk of life, you will see them in the shadows,
Always in the background until they are needed
And then they shine, to all the heroes I have ever known.

Christie Forfar

Silver Wedding

Twenty-five years ago today
You stood before God's altar,
You promised to comfort, honour and love each other
In sickness and in health.
You promised to forsake all other,
Keeping only to each other.
You promised to love and cherish,
Till death came to part you,
You gave yourselves to each other
Forever and forever.
You have kept those sacred vows,
You have never faltered.
All our love, God bless you -
To a marvellous son and daughter.

Janet Cavill

My Heart's Garden

Just for a little while I walked
In the cool of the summer night
And in the garden of my heart
Came friendship's footsteps light.
You planted within that garden
A happiness most rare -
Joy and hope and peace of mind
Were firmly rooted there.
Like the dancing lights on a river
That send back their radiance bright
I give to you the garden
I walked within that night.
I give to you my devotion
And my hand in friendship true
And the part of my heart that's a garden
Where I walk alone with you.

Joan Lewington

Innocence

It is so beautiful,
The leaf that hangs in the wind
She sails unhindered,
Piercing the air with barely a sigh
Dance, pretty leaf, dance,
You are the meaning of life, you
You are all my dreams,
And my infinite possibilities
Just you pretty leaf, just you . . .

John Chaplain

Hush

Hush, hush! Don't move the magic clock where time is now and aft
is soon forgot
Don't breathe lest fluttering branch will stir and shed the laden
cupboard store making merry
Of glossy berry, to strew the glancéd fruit where earth is bare
Whispers that shed the night from cold despair
Vista backs to vespers written, italics on thin air

Strangled life beyond the shadows creep, to steal the hoary
nights retreat
To mellow moon, resting on her ridge
Tarries on her velvet slide to mound and burrow; to find the
fluff and fur that's all tomorrow

The panoply of earth stands still to share the thrill, to hear the
silence of the soft footfall
And t'wer but just a spell when scurrying time made off, to screech
at other masters or to tell of glimmered hours untouched by frost
And still the silent sound and aft is all forgot

'Till showy spring with all her din will let the napkin drop, from
house and wall and smoking chimney pot.

Pluto

For Her

Congratulations on your divorce,
He was never your equal, of course.
I'm so pleased you ditched the creep,
He only ever made you weep.

Remember he had such smelly feet,
His dirty washing was no treat,
For what you cooked, was he grateful?
No, remember? He was truly hateful.

I know you loved him once, the snake,
But we are entitled to one mistake,
Don't waste your time reminiscing,
Get on with the life you've been missing.

Patricia Susan Dixon MacArthur

MOTHER'S DAY

Mom, you were a lovely girl,
Born in Ireland, young and pretty,
But deep inside you lurked
A longing to be free.
That longing would not go away,
'Please Daddy, let me go.'
So you crossed the deep blue Irish sea,
To a country you did not know.

A headstrong Irish lassie,
From Newry, County Down,
With friend Susan, during the war,
Settled in Oldbury town.

You may look back with some remorse
And wish that you had stayed on course,
But God mapped out a life for you,
You did not have a say.
You did your best, like all the rest.

Some times were good,
Some times were bad,
Sometimes things were really very sad.
Still you went on, stronger each day,
Paddling your own canoe
Is what you always say.

Jill Lowe

Mr Richard Antony Yappow

Dear Richard, my son,

You're 21 years old on 14th December,
I'll always remember the day you were born.
Even when my body is old and worn.
You brought sunshine, happiness and life to me,
When you were just a little boy sitting upon my knee,
Now you've grown up to be a big, big boy
You're still my pride and joy!
It won't be long before you receive your birthday present and card.
Although life has been hard
For us, still there is no need
To worry about the future or past
My love for you is made to last.
God bless you.

Love from Mum.

Teena Marie Callanan

My Son

You are so special, especially to me.
You are a wonderful person, no better could there be.
Every day is precious and happy with you around.
I feel I am so lucky, my happiness has no bounds
Now it is your birthday, I hope your wishes all come true
Certainly you deserve the best, it's long overdue.
Good health, wealth and happiness, is wished upon this day.
May your life be very happy in a very special way.

Anne Sackey

Giving Birth

The doctor stood helpless
at your coming:
needle in one hand
gas mask in the other,
giving me a choice.
But I wanted only my mother.

My mother
who would know
who had felt this terror.

Terror of a body
wracked in creation:

Drawing blood from the stone.

Drawing life from my womb.

Gis Hoyle

Our Grandchild

Many, many years have passed since first I was a bride,
Standing in a sunlit church, my husband by my side.
The future stretched before us, full of hopeful dreams,
Some of them have come to pass, and some just empty schemes.
Our children came, they brought us joy, they brought us heartache too.
But now they've gone, they've fled the nest, the way all children do.
Tonight we sit at home and wait, our anxious thoughts all torn,
To hear the news we're waiting for. Our grandchild has been born.

Marie Jaques

PRECIOUS

We've already come a long way
Shared a bumpy ride
Some pain and fear but now you're here
Forever by my side
We could spend all day together and in the night have more
Of those warm and loving cuddles that you and I adore

Sometimes I lie awake at night
With worries on my mind
I know now that won't ever stop
Such love does not unwind
To be my babe forever would be my one desire
But together we will grow apart, of me you'll doubtless tire

For now we're both discovering life
Like it's never been before
Noticing sounds, seeing lights
Rolling on the floor
Sometimes you don't say too much and I'm decoding the clues
But then I see just what you mean in those gorgeous baby blues

I have an angel in my arms
A precious, precious gift
And every time you see her
Your heart will also lift
You'll only recall beauty . . . forget evil, hurt, things vile
When Precious looks you in the eyes with her adoring smile.

Vivienne C Wiggins

BIRTHDAY CELEBRATION

My birthday was two months ago,
I celebrated it my way.
My family packed their bags and
We went on a weeks holiday.
We stayed in a static caravan
Near Bude, a lovely place.
I walked along the beach each day
With the wind upon my face.
I paddled in the sea and heard
The seagulls up above;
We picnicked every single day
With all the food I love.
And on the special day itself,
The day I was eleven,
I opened all my lovely gifts,
I really was in Heaven!
All day we spent out in the sun,
Then to Dartmoor for my tea,
And when we all got home at night,
I'd eleven candles lit for me.
I hope that all the photographs
They took of me through the day
Will remind them of the happiness
I had on my birthday.
I've had to ask my loving Mum
To write this out for me.
My paws just cannot hold the pen -
I'm a Cavalier King Charles, you see!

Ann Linney

A Sign Of Spring

A cling film sea seeps slowly back revealing stars in sand,
where heavy haze of heat hangs listless on the waking land -

The rows of rainbow-coloured huts so pristine, shine, like
ice creams out of season, locked unwanted on the promenade -

One nut brown brave his belly rippling down, hides bare beneath
his wide armed newsprint held aloft, to cultivate his tan -

Alone at hers, a primly silvered perm appears all fixed
on crochet, but with brightly shining eyes she fixes us -

The gaudy fishing boats sprawl plump and empty on the
pebble slope, their nets spread sticky wet against the drying sky -

A good night's catch and fisher folk are fingering
the slipperies with jolly jokes as we with grins and quids queue up -

The gulls unfazed by spring's surprise return are strutting booms
or perched on rocky crags to snitch their share of last night's scoop -

At Missus Bumble's tea and coffee hut the sweet-toothed sip
and guzzle treats, sunning their pinkness on the slatted chairs -

Some chirpy kids run weaving, kicking at a bouncing ball
just past the pallid sick being wheeled along for fresher air -

Then elder painted ladies teetering on clacking heels
come dragged and flushed behind their fluffy dogs from high-rise flats -

Then joggers, shoppers, families with prams, all come to see
and feel the sun, after so many weeks of wettish dull -

All blink in disbelief yet in that hazy warmth each feels
a spurt of energy in stepping out - a sign of spring -

Rosemary Keith

Mind Walking

To walk the woods and hills of yesteryears,
See again the wonders of nature's treasurers.
Ignore the ageing heart beat fears.

Walk the paths of ancient forefathers,
Along the hills of purple heather,
Rest beneath the Rowan's shade,
Watch the Red Kite swoop, and fade.

Just as he did in Merlin's days,
He who taught young Arthur his kingly ways,
And men and women lived, and loved,
In peace and honour trothed.

For thirst sip the clear crystal water,
That bubbles out the Earth.
Listen to its gentle chatter,
Echoing the tinkle of Genevieve's laughter.

Smell the dog fox in his hide,
Then see him asleep, don't hurt his pride,
Walk on, climb higher in the rocky crags,
In hidden caves the wild cat gags.

Live just a little like they did in olden times,
In your make-up some ancient genes remain,
From forebears long since forgotten.
Allow them space within your domain.

Thus the aged travel down memory walks,
No need to listen to mobile phone talks.
So when you see them sit and smile,
Walk with them along that last enchanting mile.

A R (David) Lewis

The Big 40!

Young Sam Whatsit's 40
Did you not know?
Did I hear you say
It really doesn't show?

Well, he has his own teeth
And tries to keep in shape
Goes to the gym
Limits the gin intake?

But take a closer look
Study his profile
Eyes a little glassy?
A yawn and not a smile!

A few fine lines
A sprinkle of grey hair
Little tell tale signs
Confirm some wear and tear!

But forget that you are 40
Enjoy life to the full
Age is not a barrier
No need to feel so dull!

Because 40 can be old
But 40 can be young
You are in charge
To choose which one?

Heather Denham

Reaching Fifty

You have reached the *Big Five O*
And now wonder, does it show?
As wrinkle cream is a 'con',
You can't go back and must go on.
At the age of fifty, a body *sags*
Eat a sweet, your conscience *nags*.
Print looks smaller on a page,
This is all down to your age!
Now you cannot read with ease,
And it's, 'Pass my glasses please.'

Now you're fifty, it's *hush, hush*
It brings new meaning to a '*flush*'.
At the mirror sit and stare,
When did all that *grey* get there?
Suddenly your armchair
Is more inviting than a funfair!

Yesterday you did not care
Wear a *mini skirt* you'd dare
But now you're fifty people stare!

This rhyme does not apply to you,
So please don't '*take a dim view*',
Special people like you are few,
With love this is sent to you,
Bringing all good wishes too.

Sheila Walters

That Lovely, Sharing Night

Little Josh was awakened from deep slumber
One snowy winter's night
A strange sound pierced the blackness
Again and again and more.
Sounded a bit like squeaky bunny
When he'd held her tightly before.
Just then Daddy came into his room
And swept him up into his arms,
'Come and see who's dying to meet you,
He's got all your charms.'
As they entered the bedroom,
The sound was nearer still,
Mummy's smile beamed, she seemed so thrilled!
Daddy slowly lowered Josh down, among the pillows,
He snuggled closely under Mummy's arm,
The sheets flowed like weeping willows.
How safe our Josh felt then
But wait! What was that whimpering sound?
He eased up as Mummy whispered,
'Darling look what we've found,
A brand new member for our family,
Your very own baby brother.'
He gazed in wonder at the sight
Of such a weenie infant, like no other.
Josh reached out and touched the baby hand
His little heart leapt with joy
As little fingers gripped his own, like a band.
Daddy's eyes were full of tears
At such a wonderful sight
No one thought of sleeping then, on that lovely, sharing night.

Mary Armstrong

Golden Wedding Anniversary

They came to Crown from far and near,
Some drank a short and some a beer;
To celebrate full fifty years,
Of married life, so free of fears.

Dear Aunty Jess was just so great,
Her presence truly made the date;
Both Greg and Bridget came from far,
Their very presence shone like star.

The meal itself was oh, so fine!
It really was like first class wine;
The chat and stories filled the night,
The atmosphere was all just right.

The speeches short and full of fun,
Then step outside for glimpse of sun;
The years at farm, with children young,
Brought happy memories of church bells rung.

For Golden Couple weekend the best,
Throughout the stay, life full of zest;
With midnight hour came time for rest,
The evening had been of the best.

'Twas after nine at breakfast met,
A morning walk for papers get;
Then all in lounge for coffee date,
For some 'twas time to shut the gate.

A glorious gathering coming to end,
'Twas time for thanks and love to send;
Full fifty years of love and trust,
In ten years time to gather we must.

John Paulley

ANNIVERSARY MEMORIES

Flowers fade and die away
But memories last forever
And the day that we both said, 'I do'
Is a memory I will always treasure.

For even though several years have passed
Since that very special time
The best feeling I have ever had
Is knowing that you are mine.

Nothing in my life is better
Than having you by my side
Knowing you will cheer me up
And comfort me when I cry.

For the hugs and kisses you give me
Along with your patience and endless love
Make me feel so happy and so special
And for this I thank my lucky stars and the Lord above.

But most importantly dear darling
I thank you for loving me
And for being there when I need you
I wish you a very happy anniversary!

Joanne G Castle

TESTIMONY

As a child, you were easy to find.
As a teen, I left you behind.
As a young adult in sin I was lost.
In my mid-twenties, I found the cross.

The cross on which you died for my sin,
Opened Heaven's gates and let me come in.
You forgave me and saved my soul.
I found Jesus and He made me whole.

S J Sanders

THE BIRTHDAY BARBECUE

It's barbecue season again.
The bacon is sizzling away.
The smell is just out of this world.
I wish we had one every day.

The sausages crackle and pop.
The spare ribs are browning there too.
The pork chops await their bread cakes.
There's plenty for me and for you.

The onion rings give a scent
No perfume of Paris can beat.
The stars twinkle high in the sky.
The moon shines down on those who eat.

The children run round with their spoils,
The grown-ups watch without a care.
The birthday girl skips round the fire,
The sounds of joy ring through the air.

The party food all disappears.
The work of the fathers is done.
The children all scatter indoors
To sleep till the rise of the sun.

Joyce M Turner

Chocolate

There is a little miracle I want to introduce you to,
a thing of such wonder if I'm feeling blue,
it looks so small and innocent sitting on the shelf,
enjoy it with your friends or in private by yourself.
A large box for someone close when they're feeling low,
or special ones for Mother's Day are always the way to go.

Its silky, rich texture soothes the worst of days,
or tends to a broken heart when it thinks it's love it craves.
The variety is endless, milk, plain or white,
with caramel, nuts, wafer . . . we could be here all night.
A bar in your shopping trolley as a special treat,
a slice of tempting fudge cake when you go out to eat,
it doesn't feel like Christmas without a box or two,
can also make a birthday feel really special too.

Eat them without thinking while watching TV,
or secretly pick out the best ones when you think no one can see.
Savour every one as you get lost in your favourite song,
accept the expensive box from someone saying, 'I was wrong.'

In life we need small pleasures in each and every day,
chocolate! Chocolate! I love it, I wouldn't have it any other way.

Melanie E Carty

Happy Birthday

Happy birthday Son
I'm sorry I can't be there
Because this is your special day
I would have liked to share.

God willed it this way
That we should be apart
But Son this day and always
I'll love you with all my heart.

Joan Magennis

AMOROD

'Tell me, what's an Amorod?' I enquired of my son, just three.
He raised his head with a smile that said, 'It's a word known
only to me.'
The first three syllable word he had made on his magnetic letter board
But neither in dictionary nor thesaurus could I find this word.
'What is it? What can it mean?' Such a wonderful sounding word
I think he's come up with a new one of which none of us has heard.
Could it be a small white flower, or a new power plant for cars?
Or maybe the name of the spaceship that one day will fly to Mars?
Perhaps a branch of medicine, or a new evil sort of bomb?
Who knows, it could be anything - my thoughts kept wandering on.
But no, it's a special secret word from a little boy's fresh mind
A spelling produced in innocence, with a meaning
I'm not meant to find.
But in fifty years it could appear in Webster's in The Oxford or more
But for now perhaps he'll confide in me, maybe before he's four.
So *Amorod*, a secret word you'll stay, until meaning
sometime you have
Then everyone will want one, be it fact or fad
And I'll be proud as Punch that, to his great pride and joy,
A word was added to the English language by my
own special little boy.

Mike Jackson

The Hero Of Highbridge

Frank Foley was a British spy
He was an inconspicuous guy.
No one realised to what extent
His life to many had really meant.
The excitement began from World War One
When Frank joined the army and handled a gun.
The authorities he much impressed,
As a linguist and diplomat he was a success.
He spoke German and French with such ease,
In consulate circles he aimed to please.
When the Hitler regime came to power
Frank Foley fought his finest hour.
He rescued Jews from a deathly fate
The number he saved was truly great.
A posthumous award he eventually won
Righteous Among Nations the accolade ran.
Now in his birthplace people aim
To build a statue to his name.
Highbridge in Somerset is the place
Where they plan to put this edifice.

Joyce Beard

Joey's Christening Day

(For my elder grandson)

Joseph, the starry-eyed infant
Balances a little wobble;
Rolls over, under the table.
Is ready to cry, but doesn't.

Joseph smiles quite wisely
At all the world and its foibles,
Blows out saliva bubbles
And speaks to his mum and me.

Joseph was born at Christmas
And among the snows of that month
Had no need to cut a tooth,
That started at Candlemas.

Joseph had a christening,
In his eyes the candles' light.
Six months and love holds him tight;
The world returns his smiling.

Mike Green

FOR IAN . . .

Some make complaint, the taint
    Of bitterness, maybe?
But with you, I don't feel faint
    Nor likely, e'er shall be
For you are, to me, as a saint
    For, I can surely see

That love has His home in thee:
    The One this world rejected,
And He was laid upon the tree
    That we would ne'er be . . . rejected
But held in His love's see
    That makes us, un-neglected . . .

Ian, take care dear son of God
    As in the way you turn . . . and
Help is with us, as we plod
    We find our home in His dear hand
And tho' the likes of us, is considered . . . odd,
    Yet the meek shall own this land,
And when you've time then chew this *cud*
    That builds on rock not sand!

Anon

My Dad, My Mam

My dad, my mam you are my rock
And I love you with all my heart.
Even when we are far away
We are never far apart.

Though not always together
My love for you is true.
I carry it safely in my heart
For so special to me are you.

You pick me up when I am down,
Encourage me on my way.
Give me advice which helps me through
The trials of each new day.

Thank you for all your love
When my life hit its lowest of lows.
For if I didn't have it
I could never have dealt with life's blows.

It took many mistakes,
But now I know who I am.
I can face my future with pride
Because of you, my dad, my mam.

Lynn Mottram

Truly Blessed

With silken lashes softly curled
Surpassing summer skies,
The innocence of all the world
Lies in my baby's eyes.

The wakening life to see unfold
Is love to understand,
And it's the sweetest joy to hold
My baby's dimpled hand.

She smiles at me whene'er I nurse
And does my heart beguile,
The beauty of the universe
Is in my baby's smile.

By worldly pleasures not impressed -
Let fortune disappear,
I know myself more truly blessed
To hold my baby near.

Molly Read

Our Sweetest Angel

For nine long months you were *The Bump*
That grew and grew and grew.
What would you be once you arrived?
None of us really knew.

And then that special day arrived,
You came into our world,
To share your precious life with us
A gorgeous baby girl.

Sweetest angel, you have brought,
Bright sunshine to our lives,
Bright stars to fill our darkest nights,
Bright rainbows in our skies.

There's so much love surrounding you,
So many hearts to care,
A life ahead so full of fun,
So many want to share.

We feel so proud to say that you're,
Our granddaughter so sweet,
We wish you everything in life,
You've made our lives complete.

Jim Sargant

For David, On His Birthday

No rush of love, no passion fire,
No all-consuming heart's desire,
No shuddering intake of breath,
No thought that life apart means death,
No clinging need, no jealousy,
No twisted co-dependency,
No bitterness, no mistrust,
No confusing love with lust,
No ultimatums, no commands,
Few promises and no demands,
Not quickly forged, but built to last,
Knots slowly tied, secured, fast,
We know what many never learn:
The slowest flame will longest burn.

Kate Lynn-Devere

To My Friends

I could not live without my staunchest friends
They lift me up when I am feeling low
Real friendships do not follow modern trends
As I succumb they will not let me go.
Cruel fate deprived me of a brother
So empty have I felt since that sad day.
He has gone. No longer need he suffer.
Eyes sting, head hurts. Those pains won't go away.
Good friends, great children, try to bring relief,
Some books to read, some invitations out
Their cheerful words cut through this silent grief
I need them all, of that there is no doubt.
They give their strength. They must not be left weak.
My thanks to them. Their interests now I seek.

Jenna Jackson

FAMILY

This morning my sister went into labour
I would gladly take her pain as a favour
Mind you, this is her third child
So in comparison the pain should be mild.
I have been praying every day
That mother and child will be OK
If the child is a boy he can have my name
Or take my father's, it's much the same.
I don't care, nephew or niece
My love for them will never cease
I will love to watch them grow and change
And I hope they don't turn out strange.
I hope the child is like the mother
I wouldn't change her for any other.
Oh God, watch over her please
My newest niece, little Louise.

Paul O'Boyle

LITTLE ONE

Little one, I've waited so patiently for you.
Always in my heart, I felt you near.
At one time I almost thought my feelings were untrue
and then your parents told me you were here.

My newest little grandchild, you're still a tiny mite
not yet released from in your mother's womb.
Your granny waits to cuddle you, you'll be a welcome sight
to all of us who wait within this room.

May God bless and guard your birth.
Most precious little one on Earth.

Helen Strangwige

A NICE SURPRISE

Today we received a lovely surprise
From a little girl with smiling eyes.
There in her cot she looked so good,
Her name is Kaci Hannah Collingwood.

Thank you for Kaci and we say God bless,
You look lovely there as you rest.
May God be with you every day,
And loads of luck come your way.

Out in the garden there is a dell
Where all the little fairies dwell.
Like guardian angels from above
They'll enclose you in a ring of love.

Then when they see you lying there,
For you Kaci, they'll show they care
By staying always by your side,
Never leaving you and with you abide.

May the years ahead to you be kind
And love and happiness may you find.
With all the love of family care
Nothing in this world can compare.

Francis Allen

LOVING YOU

Loving you is what life's about
It makes me want to scream and shout.

You're not perfect, don't get me wrong
But neither am I and that's what makes us strong.

I have this feeling deep inside
But when I'm with you it's so hard to hide.

We have grown together over the years
Through trials and tribulations and many tears.

We only get one life so let's make the most.
To the many years ahead, let's have a toast!

Amanda Hopley

MOTHER'S TREASURE

When I was a little child
My mother was my guide
She had so many good things to show me
And a few sad things to hide.

She was always ready to hear
She was always ready to talk.
She was always ready to sew
To go, to stay, to laugh, to walk.

She offered me two helping hands
She found me books to read
She sent me out to search every land
To find what I might need.

I looked for the perfect person
For years I continued to roam
But when I'd seen all the wonderful world
I missed what I'd left at home.

I had no need to travel on
I knew I'd stayed away too long
You never realise what treasure you've had
Until your treasure has gone.

Angela Lansbury

Flocks Of Pretty Lambs

May and it's time to appreciate sheep in the fields,
The fleecy, feeding dams and their dear little lambs,
Sunning themselves and warm, so peaceful in sleep,
But shivering and hiding in chilly winds and rain.

Spring is here with a blanket in many shades of green,
Over gardens and hedges, around the woods and farmhouses.
Beautiful scenery, Mother Nature is busy and keen.
The chestnut trees in flower, but the pollen makes us sneeze.

Thunder, lightning and hail will threaten,
Does contentment ever stay around for long?
Pretty lambs will soon be roasted and eaten,
Only glimpses to see of Heaven on this earth.

Public holidays to come and sometimes merry days,
With time to relax, take it easy, have a lie-in.
Try do-it-yourself, with elegant paper and paint,
Or have a day out, be patient on packed roads.

Children love the seaside and go running along the sand,
They build their fairy castles, digging down for treasure.
They'll be fascinated by kites that soar overland
And forget back to school and homework to finish.

Days of May will quickly vanish until another year,
It will soon be time to return to lessons and work,
Get on with the chores, they won't disappear,
But June is waiting and then summer will be here.

Sheila Rowland

SIMONE, AGED ONE YEAR TWO MONTHS

To explain to the reader
Your name ends in an *e*
Because you were born in Italy,
To a dark-eyed niece
My great nephew and heir,
You have blondie-reddish, silky hair.
Adults melt when they play with you.
Your eyes, such innocent baby blue.

You're scooped up to give us a hug
Then lowered gently on your rug.

They plonk you sweetly upon my knee
And bottle-feed you camomile tea.
For this I flew across the sea!
Italian, English, Polish; your blood.
With protective instincts
We females flood.
Little one who tugs at our heart.
In your male world
Who will play a part?
Or, like toys at the end of the day
Will we be forgotten and put away?
You'll become a man
With pride and power.
Gone - our flapping, funny flower.

Carol Sherwood

Newborn

As you lie asleep
So soft in my arms.
I gaze in wonder
At your innocent charms.

Those delicate features
That nature has formed.
The love you've aroused
Since the day you were born.

I brush my lips
To your warm pink cheek.
That sweet baby fragrance
Is the one that I seek.

Your tiny little fingers
Clasp the end of my thumb.
That great special bonding
Has already begun.

Your eyes flicker open,
You give a little yawn,
Then you go back to sleep
As a new day is born.

Dennis Young

When You Were Born

An angel sang when you were born
And her song did bless a dream
Another soul for life to share
As you sail its eternal stream.

You're the tale of a faithful wish
The rhyme of a sacred verse
You're the prayer of a union
That only love can ever nurse.

Your parents' hearts can celebrate
About their dream where you belong
Your presence does seed their happiness
That will grow as a loving bond.

This world will be your priceless stage
This moment shall be your cue
You will sense in your parents' eyes
Their love is meant for you.

David Bridgewater

Cards For All Occasions

Birthdays - anniversaries - weddings too,
Special greetings sent to you,
Get well cards - people send,
Hoping you'll soon be on the mend.

Messages sincere on a sympathy card,
Losing someone can be terribly hard,
Cards are sent to wish you the best,
When taking exams or a driving test.

A special card delivered in time,
Mother and baby both doing fine,
Moving house into a new flat,
There's even good luck cards for that.

Postcards are sent for us to say,
'Having a good time on holiday!'
A special card is on its way,
To celebrate your 50th birthday.

Even musical cards you can buy today,
When you open the card - it starts to play,
And when you reach your 100th birthday,
A telegram from the Queen is sent your way.

Trish Wright

Celebration Of Friendship

(Dedicated to Danny P McDonnell)

Fireflies flit, dancing merrily
across deep, dark December water,
to brighten a dull, misty evening;
where cold liquid laps the icy bank.

By warm muted candles and soft music,
ale pie and pasta are washed with wine,
healthily red, before cholesterol levels scream
as chocolate pudding puddles frozen full fat cream.

Mature conversation flows with happy
youthful laughter. As good friends share
a birthday meal, reflections merge
through the glass lightly.

Slowly the fairy lights are restored,
free of reflection, to sparkle an old stable,
where a mist of shire horses silently paw
the frosty earth, near rust-mangled metal;
outside *The Plough.*

Anita Richards

To My Darling Husband On Our Silver Wedding

Twenty-five years ago today
We made our happy start
Upon life's journey, hand in hand,
My darling, heart to heart.
The road has taken many a turn;
The way ahead's unsure,
But we'll be guided by the star
Of love that's strong and pure.

Patricia Fallace

Anniversary

Loving you was always easy
Hand in hand
Making our vows
The thrust of our desire
Encircled by a golden band.

Forty years on
Fashioned by faults and frailties
Tempered by respect
Honed by our love,
The circle expanded
To a comfortable maturity.

Still the caress that arouses
The look that says,
Loving you was always easy.

Vera Morrill

Antonio

My friend Antonio works at Greigo Mar
Such a pity he lives so far
When I go there, he looks after me
Having to be so careful with food, cos I'm gluten free
He always looks smart in his black suit and tie
So tall and slim he catches your eye
Excellent worker always on the go
Cos working in the restaurant, this really shows
He gets on with his work mates a real treat
Wish you could go there; he's so special to meet
Such a lovely man, a special friend
To you Antonio, my love I send.

Anne xxx

Anne Davey

Celebrating 25 Years

Our Silver Anniversary is celebrated this year.
For 25 years our school has stood here.

Our school has survived the great many hoards
Of children and teachers, and the blackboards!
We've welcomed all in with a friendly smile.
Shown them the way with books and a file!
The gift of knowledge is passed on to learn
Of sharing and caring and taking your turn.

Assemblies together; we hear the Head's words.
Discussions, debates and singing like birds!

The teaching of history on Greeks and the Romans,
The Tudors, Victorians and even the Normans.
In geography, the rivers and oceans are flowing.
Drawings of maps with the continents showing.
Religion is taught to all of the *races*,
And festivals talked of with all of their graces.
The science assignments can often be fun
Feeling good at results, when experiments are done.
There are chances for music and learning to play
Instruments of choice - you just have to say.
There's PE and drama, technology too,
Computers and cookery and artwork to view.
The importance of reading and writing are known,
That's why there's a library with books out on loan.
Fractions, percentage and learning the *time*
Division and tables - are also a crime!

The teachers work hard and all do their best
To get you through school and then through the test.

One day, when we're older, we'll turn round and look
And say, 'Our best days were spent at Bearbrook!'

Kim Kelly

Still Loving You

(Dedicated to Joyce)

It's time to celebrate again
The passing of our years,
Together we live in harmony
We have no time for tears.

Our life together is enriched
For each other we care,
Understanding our emotions
Past adversity we share.

Every new dawn is golden
Our dreams we can fulfil,
Bonding our souls together
Caressing that magic still.

A love exists between us
Which I will not deny,
From today until eternity
Our fate would not lie.

My feelings have run deep
From that first ever kiss,
Which possessed my heart
Sealing life with bliss.

Three years have gone now
Each day my love grows,
Like a never-ending river
Our romance always flows.

Forever I will be sincere
And in the years anew,
I will show my devotion
Simply by loving you.

George S Johnstone

Is This Familiar?

I like to send a birthday card
To each and every friend.
I keep a careful note of dates
And of what I choose to send.

The problem that I've found of late
Is not the clever drawing,
But finding that the words inside
Are really quite annoying.

They tend to be offensive
And occasionally smutty -
Sometimes they're idiotic -
Not funny, just plain nutty.

A picture's worth a thousand words,
So why do they gild the lily?
A cartoon with a caption neat,
Is clever work, not silly.

Because I much prefer my own
Poor efforts at some doggerel,
I buy the cards with blank insides
And write a simple verse which doesn't always work out properly.

D M Anderson

Sam

Oh dear little boy, what joy you have brought.
Your nanny melts when I see your smile
and as for your chuckle, it's greedily sought.

Grow up little Sam in the love you have given.
You will soon have your brothers to play with you, with no division.
They love you now dear Sam and protect you from all harm.

As I watch you having your daily bath,
with so much pleasure in your fragrant balm,
It gives me a feeling of warmth and wonder,
and I know my love could not be fonder

Gillian Nutbeem

DEVOTION?

At work for days and weeks on end
Miss Knox has been my constant friend.
'Be nice to me!' I once insisted
And ever since she has resisted
The urge to simply blank me out
With frigid stare or saucy pout.

At first I thought my manly grace,
My clever talk and fancy phrase
Enthralled her with demented passion
That drove her on to over-ration
Her gorgeous smiles in my direction
Convincing me of my perfection.

But then the scales fell from my eyes:
(It shouldn't come as much surprise!)
The reason for her adoration
Was not compulsive adulation.
Her earnest wish, to put it terse,
Would be to see her name in verse!

So as I write I can expect
That Cheryl's counterfeit respect
Will wither, die and I will bet
That from now on what I will get
Are haughty stares and withering looks
As I land back in her bad books!

Patrick Brady

Past And Present

The youngest girl of a large Welsh family
Born and still living in the Rhondda Valley
She is the last of that family's members
The others have gone, but always remembered.
After the grammar school she went into nursing
But not for long as she soon started courting.
In South Wales she married a wonderful man,
Settled down, enjoyed life as families can.
She worked hard, making many sacrifices
For husband and children, she had no vices.
Five children were raised in the best tradition
To teach them proper values was her mission.
Loved by all her family and relatives
And every neighbour in the street where she lives.
In her nineties now, she is always caring
In spite of her failing eyesight and hearing.
I speak, I'm sure, for my sisters and brother
A small tribute to a wonderful *mother.*

Terry Daley

Happy Birthday Loveliest Wife

Happy birthday my dearest, beautiful, loving wife
Who's more precious to me than the air I breathe.
My darling you are my very life.
When work seems hard and the world seems so full of muddles
You are there my sweetest angel, to ease away all my many troubles.
You are as fair to me as the day we first met
All those years we have spent together, I have no regrets.
I'll never stop loving you.

Ann Hathaway

ROBB'S CHRISTENING

Today is the christening of a special boy
Whose birth has given us so much joy
His hair is fair, his eyes are blue
Grandad, he makes me think of you.

It's a very proud day for his mum and dad
May God guide this little lad
Through all the dangers life does throw
That health and happiness he will know.

When we kneel to pray today
There is one thing I would like to say
When you look on your family from above
Please surround us all with your love.

Robb is now number five
How I wish you were alive
To see them all grow big and tall
But I do know you love them all.

Jill Dryden

THREE SCORE AND TEN

Since Lord of many mercies then
You grant me three score years and ten,
And more than I so much deserve
Five senses and my wits preserve,
May not my earthly life extend
Beyond sweet taste its destined end,
But let me in due time depart
With still a full and ready heart.

Barrie Williams

Roundhouse Rock

At dawn in the middle of June, with the sky dull and white as a shell
Washed up on grey pebbles, the mist hung in curtains
enclosing the way,
That gathered their gauzes and lifted like veils to the south and the west,
To clear the Byzantine translucent blue dome of a high summer's day.

The sugar-pink wild summer roses piled up in extravagant tiers:
Hedgerows heaped high overhead where the stems
of green bittersweet hide.
Along every road that we passed, flowered arches
of briars bowed down,
And sunlight spread out on the grass like the white satin
cloak of a bride.

Their scent spilling drunkenly over, awash with the promise of wine,
The elder trees brimmed and foamed over with wide
shallow goblets of flowers -
Scattering all the green paths with their tiny white papery stars:
Every warm breath of June wind brought a bushel of meteor showers.

Where the ring of great beams draws together,
up out of the firelight's reach,
High in the thatch of the Roundhouse where smoke
shadows gather above,
And years hang as heavy as incense, below the soft voice of the priest,
The shadowy air was alive with the slow conversation of doves.

Between the round hills, twilight settled - at Butser,
we beat back the night,
And danced down the earth and the ashes to stamp the date
into the floor:
When Richard and Kirsty were married, in June of 2000 AD,
We rocked the tall posts of the Roundhouse as nobody's
rocked them before!

R D Gardner

A First Grandchild

My nervousness is mounting,
Excitement fills the air.
For soon my lovely grandchild
Will be placed in my daughter's care.

Anticipation growing,
My anxiety starts to show.
I want to hold you in my arms
As I did so long ago.

For you were my first born,
A beautiful daughter, it's true.
And now your turn has come around.
I'm so very proud of you.

My heart is near to bursting.
There's so much joy to share.
Life has gone full circle
And it's me who's standing there.

I find it hard to tell you
How much this means to me.
For I am watching my girl, a mum,
With her very own family.

The greatest gift that God can give
Will soon be in your hands
As the child born at Christmas
In far off distant lands.

So cherish this precious moment,
That only new life can bring
And with the first cry of the baby,
May you hear the angels sing.

Sue Ireland

UNTIED

The rainbow's gold
your time has come
play your pipes
drum your drum.

Hear that rhythm
whirl to the beat
pound on the earth
with your bare feet.

Sing your song
spread your wings
ride those thermals
cut your strings.

Fly with the swallows
to the eye of the sun
the rainbow's gold
your time has come.

Dorothy Webb

PURE JOY

I want to shout for joy because I know that I am saved,
There is nothing else to compare to it from the cradle to the grave,
I was born again over thirty years ago but the joy it still does last,
Although it happened years ago in the distant past.
I remember it as if it were yesterday, what a joyous time it was,
I only wish you could experience it my friend because
There are no words that can describe the peace and the joy,
I never had such a fantastic day, not even as a boy.

Don Goodwin

Wedding Wishes

I wish you the brightest of summer mornings.
May the sun shine upon you by day
And the moon and the stars by night.
May the trees bear witness to your special tryst
In the waving of their branches
And may you honour and nurture each other's uniqueness.
May the blue sky mirror the depth and the openness between you.
May nature share with you her beauty.
May your guests bring you the joy of eternal friendship
And may you all come together to celebrate with music and song.
May the wind and the trees and the sun and the moon
And all the stars of Heaven sing with you
And may the loving and the singing of that day and that night
Go on inside you forever.

Chris Woodland

Dad

No card to buy, no gift to send,
For where you are you cannot be reached,
But I will remember you on your special day,
Just like I used to before you went away.
You were a very special dad,
The best that I could ever have,
Each year that passes, I miss you so,
I wish that you didn't have to go,
But that is how it has to be,
God bless,
Happy Father's Day.

M Wills

Our Mam

Our mam was kind, our mam was good.
Our mam did everything she could
to wash us, clothe us, feed us too
to love us, but chide us when she had to.
Having seven of us children to do this for,
she was a 'blooming miracle' as our dad saw.

I was the youngest of our mam's brood
and sixty years on, still recall her mood.
When she sang a lullaby or comic song
such a sweet, gentle voice - but really strong.

I still hear her whisper, 'Goodnight, God bless'
I would say, 'Are you still there, Mam?'
and she would answer, 'Yes!'

Nowadays, when I think of our mam,
I close my eyes and see her pushing John's pram.
This is a very old memory, for John is my son
aged well over 33.

D M Letchford

Accelebation

I send you love for this happy day,
Wishing everything goes your way,
And hoping your smile will shine throughout,
Lighting the hearts of all about,
And praying luck will not leave your side,
But embrace you in a warm delight,
For you deserve perfection in everything,
For you achieve it in yourself.

Helen Marshall

This Special Day

This special day is just for you and I
Another year for us has gone on by
But each day is special in its way
The joy of life I share with you each day.

Tender moments I recall, with the world at our feet
Magic times when life was gentle and sweet
And how we weathered each tempest, each storm!
Saw it through, and old love was re-born.

My only one you are for ever more
When love was young I didn't feel so sure
But our love has stood the test of time
Now, for evermore, you will be mine.

This special day is yours and mine
How I love to see your love light shine
A lifetime of caring and sharing gone by
This special day is just for you and I.

Karl Jakobsen

Happy Birthday

I'm so pleased today is your birthday
For it enables me to say
What a pleasure it is to know you
Whilst travelling on life's way.
All the very best in the future
For your health and happiness I pray,
But meantime it's your birthday
So *glad rags* on, let's go make hay!

E Marcia Higgins

Angel Sweet

Go to sleep
My angel sweet
And dream sweet dreams
While you're asleep
Your daddy will
Be home quite soon
Perhaps the early afternoon.
It's been a year
Since he's been gone
He'll be surprised
How much you've grown
You'll smile the way
You always do
And you will
Captivate him too.

Jeanette Gaffney

The Shape Of Things To Come

You've got the sweetest little blossom
Lying in your arms
Waiting to beguile you with his many charms.
Cupid lips for kissing - dimple in his chin
If ever he is wicked you will never win.
He'll twist you round his finger
Then send you round the bend
Will make you ask the angels
'Whatever did you send?'
Dirty hands and snotty nose
Holes in socks to show his toes
Scabby knees and dirty collar
Yes! You will love your fella.

D Adams

CONGRATULATIONS

A baby is the greatest gift
That you will ever own
A precious one to have and hold
He'll bring you joys unknown
With tender times when you will fondly
Look upon his face
The tiny mouth, eyes and nose
His honours you will praise
And when his fingers grip you tight
So small and yet so strong
He's telling you in his own way,
'Now I too belong.'
The part that was your own
Will never be again
For captured is your heart and mind
Forever and all time.

Gloria Aldred Knighting

MY SPECIAL DAY

First thing in the morning,
butterflies in my tummy.
Then the excitement kicks in,
from then on the day goes so fast.
All the people there for us.
Then I become worried,
having to say all those words
in front of everyone.
What happens if it comes out wrong?
Then before I know it, it's over.
I'm now married and all the feelings
have floated away, except for happiness.

Victoria Nash

GOLDEN DAY

Through special days
From silver, pearl and ruby,
We've marked the years
With celebrated joys.
And now we've reached
Yet one more special milestone
Our golden day
Of memories we've shared,
Such happiness and love
The years have given,
To bless us,
As we gather on this day,
To celebrate
And share our joys with others,
On our truly happy,
Special *golden day.*
Those looking forward
May they have
Such years as ours to treasure,
As we join those
Now looking back
On happy years, full measure . . .

Joan Hammond

THE ANNIVERSARY

A mossy stone, a quiet churchyard, overgrown
So forgotten, so neglected and so unmown,
A mother left in sorrow there, the very best
And nothing better there to mark her from the rest.

Birthday flowers, fresh, an anniversary,
For how many years, arranged so carefully,
They never seem enough to give, however spent
We should have raised her a marble monument.

In happier days we often came this way
And never dreamt we'd come alone to pray
Oh, would the grief be less, what could we do?
We wanted something grander far for you!

E Hawkins

My Days With Dad

It was in the nineteen-thirties when the start of this takes place
And I can well remember those early days with grace,
My father taught me many things a young boy needs to learn
The rights and wrongs of what to do without being too stern,
Oft' whilst in my childhood days we'd walk for miles the country ways
There was always lots to see, he taught me to go silently,
So's not to scare those dwellers of the wood
And see the squirrels who so often stood,
High up in the branches of those lofty trees
Where, in autumn, leaves fall softly in the breeze.
Sssh there's a mother starling by her nest
And quietly we would sit and rest,
To let her feed her young ones free from fear
No harm would come to them whilst we were here.
Sometimes when the days looked fine, we'd go off with rod and line
To fish and dig for bait, beside the river bank for hours we'd wait,
But those peaceful days of pleasure were drawing to a close
The threat of war was drawing near, dad donned his service clothes,
No more to take our pleasant walks along the country lanes
The peace and silence shattered with the noise of guns and planes.
But luckily throughout the war, with all its fears and dread
Me with both my parents did share our Christmas spread,
My childhood days were passing throughout those years of strife
And thinking of those carefree days with our happy country life.
So if I'm ever low and everything seems bad
His memory brings me courage of my one and only dad.

Anthony Williams

My World

All that your eyes can survey
All that your mind can hold
Don't approach me with caution
Just because you can't relate to my world
I was born in a poor village in Trinidad
I was raised in a violent home
My mind was injured and fractured
My heart was broken and torn
But I learned my lessons well
From all the things I was never taught
From the people I learnt not to be like
I have broken the cycle
I have grabbed hold of the mike
And declared to the world
This may be my past - but it's not my future
I will create my mould
Look at me now
Healed and ready to take on the world!

Kiechelle Degale

Little Andrew Toms

No one can ever ease the pain
When one we love has died;
Anger burns within the soul
With grief no place to hide.

Yet in the depths of grief and pain
One truth gives us the strength
To know our love made up in height
What it sadly lacked in length.

Our grief is shared at this sad loss
But time will not erase
The memory of the lad whose smile
Lit up his entire face.

So come the day when we unite
The angels they will say . . .
'Daddy Toms, we told you he
Was just a hug away.'

Linda Zulaica

The Jubilee Celebrations

The children came out of school and went up the street,
To the community hall for a special treat,
The flags were flying high above the busy road,
Tables in the big hall were laden down with food.
Mums and dads and other folk were in the hall,
Everyone had come along to really have a ball,
Singing, dancing, jokes and stories were readily told,
The elderly related things that happened in days of old.
Food was eaten, drinks were drunk, everyone enjoyed the spree,
They had all come along to celebrate our Queen's Jubilee.
The national anthem was sung to commemorate the years,
After which the organiser requested three hearty cheers.
Every child was given a Jubilee mug to add the final touch,
All of the people said they had enjoyed the celebration very much.
The party closed, they all went home to jump into their beds,
Happy but tired and ready to just rest their weary heads.

Stan Gilbert

Ing

It's their wedding morning,
They can't sleep, it's just dawning,
The birds are singing,
A few hours later the church bells will be ringing,
The bride's mother's mothering,
The bride feels like she's smothering,
The groom's best man is helping,
The dog's shut outside yelping,
The wedding cars are arriving,
Chauffeurs are driving,
Presents the guests are carrying,
In the church the vicar is marrying,
At the reception the best man's speaking,
The bridesmaid's new shoes are squeaking,
The bride and groom are kissing,
Soon they will be missing,
The band is playing, the crooner's crooning,
Soon the lovers will be honeymooning,
The last of the guests are leaving,
It's been a lovely day and a lovely evening.

Richard Trowbridge

A Birth

A miracle happened in Heaven above
This baby was sent for you to love
A little one to cherish, a creation so new
Bringing joy and happiness through and through
The angels celebrate in Heaven, it's true
For your special arrival they chose . . . just for you
Congratulations are sent to you on this day
To celebrate your little miracle in every way!

Jo Hodson

My Stunning Bride

(Positano, 21st September 2002)

In love's fair house my heart is found
Its married beat to you is bound
Your simplistic beauty and complex mind
Make you my love my greatest find
As time moves on and is forever changing
Our plans for life we are just arranging
They start today as we wed
Combining vows often said
The difference being our hearts' desire
Only honest love do we require
Today we celebrate our affirmation
And true love smiles at its new creation
Forever long last this love inside
For today my dear you are my stunning bride.

Darren Taylor

I Only Have Myself To Blame!

I remember I was angry, I really knew not why.
Anger took a grip on me and I let a friendship die.
My anger lasted several years, in that time I took no blame.
I've just realised where the problem lay and I hang my head in shame.
Having a lack of social skills and a very suspicious mind
I misinterpret comments and to meanings I am blind.
I knew not how to rectify but she did it graciously.
She walked along the garden path then gently smiled at me.
Away went all the anger and with it went the grief.
She gave me back her friendship and a very sweet relief.
'Twas then I said my sorry and we chatted for a while.
She took away my big mistake with a warm and gentle smile . . .

Rosie Hues

A Surprise

It's my birthday, think I'll celebrate,
I'm fifty, yes it's true,
My other half gives me a card,
Says, 'What would you like to do?'

'Shall we go out to a restaurant,
Have an expensive bottle of wine?'
He busies himself on the telephone,
Comes back and says, 'That's fine.'

I take a nice long bubble bath,
Wash my hair and do my nails,
I look inside my wardrobe,
Take some outfits from the rails.

I choose a smart new outfit,
He shouts, 'It's time to go!'
A quiet meal, just the two of us,
He does his best I know!

We drive up to the restaurant,
He says, 'Go right on in,'
The lights go on and voices shout,
'Surprise!' I need a gin!

My family and my friends are there
To help me celebrate,
There's a cake and dancing, what a night!
Being fifty is just great.

June Melbourn

A Poem For Our Newborn Baby

We didn't know what you were going to be
A mixture of your dad and me
Fit and healthy is all that we asked
For Mother Nature, a menial task.

So proud to be your mum and dad
When we finally held you
So warm and glad
A feeling that's totally unique.

To have you here, to hold you tight
To sing you songs in the dark of night
The love you will receive will be second to none
Those growing days, those times of fun.

We will love you more
Than you could need
Keep you warm, protect and feed
You'll always be our baby.

It was a waiting game you had to play
There's one more thing that I'd like to say
A bond was born many months ago
A mother's job is quite hard you know.

To see your eyes, your face and smile
We had to wait for just a while
We love you, we love you, we always will
Our newborn baby, oh what a thrill!

Craig Lethan

The Dress

(To celebrate Kathryn's wedding - 25th August 2001)

'Midst all the flurry and excitement of the day,
The nerves and sweating palms there must have been.
There is but one instant, which was for me, when time stood still
And tears and emotions took hold and bade me stop and think;
My daughter was to wed and this was to be her dress.

It hung so empty in the window space
In her room which, for nearly twenty years she had filled
With toys and tears, and laughter too; she worked,
Her books stacked until they touched the ceiling.
But not today; today the die was surely cast.

The white did not appear so bright as it would tomorrow;
The needlework so beautifully embroidered mirrored
On the wedding orders of service now began to spring to life.
This was my daughter and she was leaving home;
To be cared for and loved by another.

I could not speak; my eyes were full and my throat so tight
That I just stared; glad to be alone in the room and in the house.
This was my little girl; my eldest daughter;
Confident and strong but fragile and tender in such a situation
And I had to be her escort until tomorrow.

Joined by friends and sister, the dress took on life;
Purity and simplicity walked down the stairs that day,
Giving me unbound joy and filling my heart with love.
Such beauty; such delight would shine today on all around
And I would walk with pride to give my girl away.

The journey there was like a magic carpet ride in style,
The people who had gathered, I did not really see,
It was in church that all the eyes turned to take in the scene
And share with us the joyful realisation of marriage
The culmination and commitment of the happy pair to be.

No human thoughts can explain just how a father feels,
Maybe it's just sentimentality or being plain soft;
But the sight of that gorgeous dress brought it home to me
Time has moved on and it is time for you to spread your wings;
To make you home, with the one you love, as I did years ago.

Trevor Huntington

ALL WORTH IT

As I inflate the balloons, I wait for you to arrive,
Pray that you enjoy your present, it is a big surprise.
An air of silent expectation fills the sitting room,
Party banners make everything bright, lifts mundane gloom.

Huge quantities of food rests arranged on paper plates,
Slowly seconds tick on 'til party time, starting at eight.
Have I invited enough guests to make the do go with a swing?
Looking, I wonder if I have forgotten anything?

Musical doorbell chimes and the first of the guests are here,
While all of my deep fears, as you walk in, soon disappear.
Wonderment look on your face, is one of pleasure and glee,
Admire all you see, including the love of your life - me!

Then it's on with the latest music, have frenetic dance,
Even though I'd like to chat with you, I do not get the chance.
Many hours later as the last guests finally depart,
You utter the magical words which gladden my old heart.

'Please believe me, this was my best birthday party ever,
Will treasure it, savour each moment, forget it never.'
And the hard work I had done had been worth all the effort,
Now all that was left before bed, was a last glass of port.

S Mullinger

Darwin's Baby

I'm waiting for a baby, not mine but for my daughter
At forty, this her third, she wants it under water
I know it is quite fashionable to do it now like this
But is it really natural to give birth like a fish?

Then I think of evolution - we pass through Pisces so they say
With a phase of nearly gills early in the day
Of the months of embryology as baby grows its way

So I suppose . . .

To the underwater genera we are sort of related
Darwin's tale of evolution must not be underrated
Then again the baby's carried in an ante-natal fluid
In fronded folds of membrane, draped like an ancient druid.

When a birth is started by a trigger quite miraculous
And the boy or girl is born and steadily looks back at us
It breathes the air and cries and everyone's exalted
But if it is submerged, the response is briefly halted
Until it softly surfaces, then plucked from naissance water
Gives reassuring signs of life. This is Genevieve, a daughter.

And so it ended happily, tho' seventeen days late
At 10lbs the family's heaviest, (that is so far to date)
The cord was stretched to breaking just before the birth
And big sister Lily's news at school provided sweetest mirth.

'My mum has had a baby,' (solemnly this is spoken)
'In a bath, I've got a sister, but the chain got broken!'

V Jean Tyler

Miss

I see each sunrise in her eyes
That happy laugh within her lies
When she sleeps I watch her breathe
This child of hope I will not leave.

If she is hurt or starts to cry
Shall I be there the pain to buy
I cannot stand to hear the tears
From a child of hope of just six years.

My little girl in every way
So alien to my macho play
And when she puts her hand in mine
I see the trust held in this sign.

My life I know she will enhance
Her grace still awkward in her dance
A confidence that's not quite set
This child of hope no cares beset.

Yet when she sits to comb her hair
That elegance is not quite there
But it will come of that I'm sure
To a child of hope on life's first tour.

And if some day she leaves my side
To see the world or make a bride
I will be there when she comes home
To a quiet love that's set in stone.

J P Worthy

WEDDING MEMORIES - FIFTY YEARS ON

The cameras' shutters click
Transfixing images forever,
To be viewed with fascination
By succeeding generations.

Mother, elegant in blue
Adjusts her hat on coiffured hair
Exuding calm she does not feel.
Marshals bridesmaids to the car.

Bridesmaids, a froth of pink organza
A-flutter with a chill excitement,
Feel at once both strange and solemn,
Whirl away. The day's begun!

The bride descends into the hall
Trailing beauty and white lace.
Father waiting takes her hand.
How soon the years have come to this!

Expectation like a perfume
Permeates the vaulting spaces.
Organ swells into a thunder.
The groom has turned to greet his bride.

There together at the chancel
Vows are made and rings exchanged;
An ancient rite touched by enchantment.
Permission given to *kiss the bride.*

Brownie guard of honour frames
The pictures which recall that day.
Amid the laughter and the bustle
Two people wrapped in their own world.

B J Chamberlaine

Pop! Pop! Pop!

Pop! Pop! Pop! The champagne corks
On this great occasion,
We are celebrating oh!
Join our jollifications!

Let us all rejoice
With the whole wide world.
Pop them here, pop them there,
Pop them everywhere!
Pop! Pop! Pop!

Pop them for all hopes fulfilled
Pop them for love obtained,
Pop for peace and all goodwill,
And all that we have gained.

Let us all rejoice
With the whole wide world.
Pop them here, pop them there,
Pop them everywhere!
Pop! Pop! Pop!

Pop them for all health and joy,
Pop them for friendships dear,
Pop them for good gifts galore,
And for all, far and near.

Let us all rejoice
With the whole wide world.
Pop them here, pop them there,
Pop them everywhere!
Pop! Pop! Pop!

Joan Egré

WILL YOU

Will you call for me?
My picture placed for you to see.
For my voice will you intently try to hear
And stare morosely at your beer?
Will your arms still ache to hold
Embrace me with your love enfold?
Will your eyes strain to seek
Missing me by hour and week?
Will your tears slowly fall
And memories of us hold you enthral?
Will pictures of the past still play
Of when our love was here to stay?
Will you speak of me with pride
And hold the remnants of our love inside?
And will you reach to hold my hand
And still remember, still understand?
Will you call my name out loud
Still listening for my every sound?
Shall my face instantly be recalled?
My touch like the gentle covering of a shawl?
Will you call for me
When I am no longer here for thee?

Emma Gascoyne

SHEER JOY

Little one so precious, so new
Family and friends waiting for you
A home so full of love
For you like an angel from above.

Your tiny hand, your raven hair
Your nose, your lips, so perfect there
You open your eyes to view the world
As we stare at this miracle unfurled.

Little Grace - oh little one
Like a ray of golden sun
You lighten the world like the promise of spring
Or the bells that herald a new year in.

The wonder of birth is one to behold
Our generation is now growing old
Yet in you we live eternally
'Cause you're a part of your grandad and me.

Ann Oliphant

JESSICA

You were always there when I needed a friend,
You were someone on whom I could always depend.
You came with me to my father's grave,
You were totally unselfish and always forgave.
You'd listen to me going on and on -
But I woke up this morning and saw that you'd gone.
I got a sick feeling deep down inside,
I felt as if someone had ripped my heart open wide;
I never appreciated you when you were here,
But now that you've gone it's blatantly clear,
How important you are - a part of my life.
You've been with me in good times, helped me through strife.
You were a friendly face, a sociable drink,
And now you're not here, it's made me think
Of how special you are - how much you meant,
I took you for granted before you went.
It may sound contrived, but it's not - it's true
- I mean it, Jessica - I really miss you.

Nicola Sheehan

Coming Of Age

It only seems like yesterday
when you were just a boy.
We'd laugh and play together
and sometimes you'd annoy.

You'd climb up trees and scrape your knees
and chase the cat so carefree.
If anyone had done you harm
they'd have to answer to me.

The things you liked and didn't like
these, only I would know.
I never thought in all that time
how quickly you would grow.

But suddenly I look at you
at eighteen, tall and strong.
That little child has waved goodbye
and grown into a man.

Although the parting is so sad
the future must go on.
And no mother could be prouder
than I am of you, my son.

Sandra Smith

Love So Deep

Just as the dolphins swim together
So our love binds us together.
Our love is as deep as the deepest ocean,
Our love is as mighty as the most powerful ocean.
Just like the tide that must keep on flowing
So will our love just keep on growing.

Zandra Collisson

Needham Lake In Suffolk

A walk around Needham Lake is the perfect place to be,
lots of happy faces, lots to do and see.
As the sun beats down I try to catch some rays,
it's so peaceful here, I could stop here for days.
A swan exits from the water and expands its pearly wings,
a mallard by its mother opens up its beak and sings.
Five yellow baby chicks go bobbing up the stream,
with Mum keeping check there is six in her team.
The climate is increasing as I'm topping up my tan,
I'm thinking of an ice cream from the ice cream van.
Now the sun is fading, it's time to think of home,
parents begin to pack away, children start to moan.
I've really enjoyed today, I'll be back very soon,
nothing is planned for tomorrow, I'm back here after noon.

Lorraine Hunting

Draw Close

Draw close to me my precious one
Don't shy away or stall, just come!
I see your pain and broken heart
The lonely sorrow, regrets that smart!
I feel your aching, hear your cries
Sense your hurt 'midst silent sighs,
There's nothing you need do or say
I understand in *every* way.
Just come to me, rest in my love
Draw comfort from your God above
For in *me* lies this blessed hope . . .
Eternal life and strength to cope!
So draw close child, please heed my call
Give me your pain, your grief, your *all*!

E S Dean

THE GOLDEN YEARS

It was April the 12th when we were wed:
My bride carried carnations, they were red,
A bright sunny day, not a cloud in the sky,
Our day went so well, without a sigh.

After scrimping and scraping, in '56 we bought a car,
A Y-type Ford, albeit on a shoestring it took us far,
February 9th 1958 in Kettering Hospital St Mary's
Paul arrived, mother and baby well, matron contrary!

We battled life's way but progress was very slow,
So decisions were made, Lilford farming must go,
Oundle beckoned with a cottage, so off we went,
Working at Perkins in Peterborough to pay rent.

Time rolled by; we celebrated our 25 silver years,
A party with lots of dancing, laughter and cheers,
Scott Gibbin Ltd, the work place, to earn my crust,
We continued dancing together! That was a must.

Watching cricket was another favourite pastime,
Had quite a few old cars; but only one at a time,
Time for another good party, Paul's 21st birthday,
Music and dancing, food and wine fit for the day.

Forty years passed by; glad rags on, it was party time again,
Highgate Hall, Elton, went on till goodness knows when,
Far away from food rationing, when first we settled down,
Now supermarkets full of delicious food, in every town.

With support from our families and friends new and old,
This was our fiftieth, *yes*, to celebrate our year of gold,
We have seen lots of changes, not always for the better,
Only ten more and our Queen will send her royal letter.

Reg Winfield

MOUNTAINS

There is a mountain to climb,
And we have given it the name of life,
There are different ways to conquer it,
In victory, defeat, hardship and strife!

Gotta have the stamina and grit,
To scale the dangerous climb,
Gotta take it on the chin,
When 'Life' covers you with its grime.

Maybe every day might not be perfect,
Maybe you'll fall a metre or two,
Sometimes you will feel on top of the world,
Some other days you might not be able to see it through.

Some days you'll meet the unexpected,
A friend or foe or a hot-legged lover,
Some days could be full of hate or love,
Some days seem to last forever.

Some people are given a head start,
Through money or political power,
Some people never get far,
Some may never see their finest hour.

Some people are content to achieve so little,
Some people are never fulfilled,
Some people are happy to help each other,
Some people quarrel and get killed.

So after all the struggle and torment,
To reach higher and higher,
Our medal of honour will be our tombstone,
Congratulations, therefore, words of a liar.

Darren Hobson

Poem For Poppy Day

The poppies they grow in the fields, a bright red
To remind us of our young men who were shot down dead
Remembrance day is nigh, is at hand
And will be held at cenotaphs throughout the land
Made into wreaths, poppies will be sold
For men who died for our country, so I've been told
Remember all you people, remember the dead
The young men who were shot through the body and head

Two wars they fought that this country would be free
And not under the yoke of any tyranny
The young and the old they gave up their lives
And left behind grieving orphans and wives
We will remember them now we are growing old
Many have died from war wounds so I have been told
While men live free and are at peace
Will this dying of wounds ever cease?

But we will remember the sacrifice they made
To die by bullet or the bayonet blade
So the cenotaph will be used once a year
To honour the men we all hold so dear
Their suffering and their death of dying in pain
Wasn't after all a death in vain
For we now have peace all over the land
The remembrance is of you, is thc poppies of England.

E A Gentles

For A Friend On His 90th Birthday

They say that three score years and ten
Is man's lifespan, I'm told.
Today you're four score years and ten -
By golly, you are bold!

I would have sent you flowers,
If I'd known they wouldn't vex;
But they were too expensive
And, besides, you're the wrong sex!

Roger Williams

YOU TWO

Two little Chinese figures, or are you Japanese?
You sit upon the mantelpiece, and the dust it makes me sneeze,
That you have gathered through the years, in your every
nook and cranny,
We dust you off as best we can, but can't compete with Granny.

Who must have owned you at some time, in your very long-lived life,
I've often sat and wondered, if you were man and wife,
When you were made all those years ago, certainly as a pair,
Hands on laps, sat so proud, each on your own chair.

I love to sit and admire you, in your almost regal gowns,
But why the solemn faces? Yes, why have you both got frowns?
Is there something in your past, that's made you look so sad?
You're only china ornaments so it can't have been that bad.

I love your hats, yes, both are great, in their individual way,
But what's that on the top of yours Sir? Well I wouldn't like to say,
It looks like a propeller, oh no, I'm not mocking your attire,
Why, it's the oriental influences, which makes the west inspire.

Yes, even David wears a sarong, no not me, I mean Beckham,
Well he did a while ago now, but it wasn't cool in Peckham,
So cheer up, smile, yes try and force yourself to grin,
And take all this life has to give, yes, take it on the chin.

David Downie

New Parent

The wonder of new birth,
A baby more than worth
The sweetest thing on Earth.

A privilege indeed
To cherish and to feed,
To meet him in his need.

An opportunity
To nurture life and free
A personality.

A duty for his sake
To give as much as take,
A life to make or break.

Janet Forrest

Pink Rabbits

Whenever her birthday comes into mind
And I think of her meaning to me
I go to the shop where I know I will find
A verse and a gift - like a knee -

Jerk type reaction, this seems the attraction
In loving anyone at all -
So just stop and think, is she worth buying pink
Bloody rabbits, or best not to fall.

Peter Asher

To My Wife . . .

They say time flies when you're having fun
and that I can vouch is true,
because it doesn't seem 12 months ago
I last said 'Happy Birthday' to you.

I'm not only wishing you a happy day
but counting my own blessings too,
and thinking of how lucky I am
for every day I spend with you.

You've made me happier than I could wish
with all the things you do,
so I guess what I really want to say
is thank you for just being you.

Kriss Simone

I Saw Her Walking

I saw her walking, walking by
The girl in the picture really held in my mind's eye
So I ran outside yet could not see
She had really walked away from me.

I saw her walking, walking by
About midday I wonder why
Just where was she going to?
Just somewhere upon this street, out of my view.

I saw her walking, walking by
Am I daydreaming in my lunch hour?
Is it like her or is it not
Or of my dream last week have I really forgot?

Keith L Powell

ON YOUR SPECIAL DAY

When children receive an invitation
They glow with excitement and anticipation.
It's a chance to wear their best bib and tucker
To feast like a gourmet, enjoy fun, games and laughter.
Cards in coloured envelopes drop through the letter box.
Ruth with her ringlets is as fair as Goldilocks,
Pretty as a picture in tartan taffeta and patent shoes.
Come on. There isn't time to lose.
Her friends are gathering at the village hall
Bearing gifts like Magi, one and all.
A puppy could have a paper chase
As wrappers, tags and ribbons fall apace
To reveal toys, trinkets and bibelots.
Blossoms from forest, field and hedgerow,
Matching serviettes and tablecloths, tinkling china,
Doilies, balloons make this an occasion to remember.
Mothers serve bread rolls with savoury fillings
Then trifle and cream in generous helpings.
After meringues, eclairs, Ruth blows out the candles.
The birthday cake will be taken home in parcels.
There is a sing-song while fathers move the furniture.
Then all are seated to play Spinning the platter.
A-hunting we will go, musical chairs and forfeits
Are followed by entertainment, magic and puppets.
Soon it will be time to say, 'Thank you for having me.'
Twilight's shadows lurk near brook and tree.

Now your birthday activities may be rather more sedate.
Time and tide for no man wait.
I wish you happiness on your special day
Many blessings in a beautiful bouquet.

Vivienne Brocklehurst

REUNITED

They took him away from me,
I cried and pleaded in vain,
I was too young, they said,
or couldn't they bear the shame?

Each birthday, a reminder,
of the day I let him go,
for six whole weeks I held him,
and how I loved him so.

But I wasn't fit, they said,
new parents took him home,
I've spent so many years,
longing for him alone.

Now the longing could be over,
the letter held tight in my hand,
I wait, in hope, with a little fear,
hoping he will understand.

I want to run away and hide,
what am I doing here?
But soon this stranger's by my side,
and all my fears just disappear.

He puts his hand in mine,
his eyes wet with tears,
he kisses me so tenderly
and cancels out those lonely years.

Now we face the world together,
love has overcome our fears,
mother and son reunited,
looking forward to future years.

Margaret Meadows

SOULMATES

The days when we laughed together are long gone.
The nights when we lay together are now done.
All that is left is the memory of your face
And a heart that is nothing but an empty space.
When we were together we could not be beat.
United we had the whole world at our feet.
We stuck by each other through thick and thin.
Whatever the problem, we knew we could win.
We rode high on the waves of passion and love,
Sometimes reaching the stars in the sky above.
You took me to places that I'd never been,
And showed me many things that I'd ever seen.
The years, they passed by. In the passage of time
We started a family. Our whole world was fine.
The children grew up and left - just you and me.
Together, alone. Another chance to be free.
We discovered our youth in a lot of ways
And strengthened the bond made in earlier days.
But now you are gone. Our time came to an end,
And I've lost my soulmate. My only true friend.
But I know that one day our two souls will meet.
For a love as strong as ours cannot be beat
By time or distance or the parting of hearts.
We'll continue with our love, which here did start.
And then once again, we'll ride high on our love,
Exploring the landscapes of the world above.
Together, forever, till the end of time,
I will be yours, my love, and you will be mine.

Cari Hilaire

Babies

Babies are born every minute of every day,
The strange fact is that unless related to you,
The number of children born leaves you non-plussed,
That information is as dry as dust.

But along comes Johnnie or is it Jane?
Bursting to tell you their good news,
So excited are they at the prospect
Of tiny feet running through their domain.

They can't wait to tell their parents,
Who are just as pleased as can be,
The ladies discuss the pros and the cons,
Of knitting or buying for the yet to be born.

Will the baby be a boy or a girl?
Pink for a girl, blue for a boy,
Take no chances, use yellow, white or green,
The baby won't care the colour, but be a bundle of joy.

The grandads will do their bit as befits,
A wooden cot wouldn't go amiss, so
Get out your tools and get cracking,
Think ahead, a wooden train with a shrill whistle.

To announce the comings and goings every day,
But stop! Think! Are they thinking too far on?
Mapping out the pleasures in life,
To be gained from caring for this child, not yet born.

Mary Lawson

MY SISTER'S GETTING MARRIED

My sister's getting married
and it's awful news,
my sister wants a page boy
and it's me she's going to choose.

She's going to buy a satin suit
with frills and lacy stuff,
a soppy little jacket
with soppy little cuffs.

I'm going to be a page boy
but please don't tell my mates,
don't tell 'em where the church is
don't tell 'em the wedding date.

Oh please don't tell 'em
I wish it wasn't true,
my sister is 27
and I am 42.

David Sheasby

NEW GENERATIONS

New generations are evolving
Taking the breath of life everyday
All that's in the air, sea or land
Yield forth the presence of Heaven and Earth
Rejoicing in the beginning
In the beginning of a world
That's always new.

P Ismail

A Golden Girl

I'm going to be a golden girl,
Because I admire the Queen.
Fifty years upon the throne,
A Monarch great she's been.

Some subtle golden low lights,
Put into my greying hair.
Yes, on June 2nd I'm going to glow
But what am I going to wear?

A golden top and a golden skirt,
My golden rings and chains,
And I'll buy a golden brolly,
Just in case it rains.

Alex will wear his golden tie,
I bought in Debenhams,
I know he'll wear it with aplomb,
And keep it out of the crumbs.

Golden sandals on my feet,
Gold knickers - where to buy?
I might have to make do with red - white or blue,
But to be a golden girl - I'll try.

In future years when we reminisce,
And backwards our thoughts will stray,
I shall remember being a golden girl,
If only for a day - June 2nd 2002.

Pamela Carder

God Gave Me The Wisdom To Help You Grow

And when I die
The rivers will flow
The sun will shine
The grass will grow

You'll be strong
With a heart so true
Filled with lessons
I taught to you

You're never alone
You never will be
I prayed for angels
To watch over thee

This is life
This is love
I'm with God in Heaven
Watching you from above.

Kathleen Nelson

For My Daughter Mo

(Married in Sri Lanka - October 22nd)

These words I write are special
They're written just to say
Congratulations Mo and Keith
On this, your wedding day.

I know that we are miles apart
But thoughts are all of you
May your lives be long and peaceful and
All your dreams come true.

As you travel on life's highway
Down your chosen path
May love and happiness be with you
And last your lifetime thro'.

Eleanor Margaret Brooks

ANNIVERSARY

(Dedicated to my dearest husband Rodney)

The time has swiftly flown
Oh where have they gone, those fifty years?
We have shared joy in abundance
Also shed many tears.
God gave us two children to love and cherish
Through good times and storms of alarms.
I felt so very blessed
When I held them in my arms.
You are my soulmate and my friend
Our love remains in heavenly bliss
As these golden years unfold
I remember our first kiss.
We now find we are laughing
At the things we do and say
Am I going out tomorrow
Or should I have gone yesterday?
Fifty years of memories
Gently they unfold
Please God don't let this world demolish
Into oblivion and lose other folks' years of gold.
Because like phoenix rising from the ashes
Our love will forever hold.

June Jefferson

Two Different Days In April

Have I enjoyed two different days?
You bet I really have,
I've just had my umpteenth birthday,
My friends have made me so glad.

This was my first day with one of them,
A trip to a market town,
The market was in full swing there,
But the rain came pouring down.

But never mind, the object was,
To visit a Wiltshire cathedral,
With a wonderful spire and old stone floors,
We mingled with all kinds of people.

Trip number two was just as grand,
In Devon down on the moors,
The daffodils out, the trees so tall,
We went to beautiful Becky Falls.

The water was going over boulders so huge,
You stop and stare in awe,
Nature in all its glory,
Who could ask for more?

They let me choose these birthday treats,
From memories you never part,
Two different days in April,
I'll keep within my heart.

So I'm glad my birthday is springtime,
Although I'm well past my prime,
I thank friends for those special days out,
And God for this precious time.

Rachel Mary Mills

YOUR FRIEND NAT

My name is Nat
And I live in a little flat
With the longest address
In the world.

My name is Nat, the bargain queen.
Watch out for the 'Natmobile'
But you won't see me
Above the steering wheel!

My name is Nat,
I may be small
But I'm good
At cycling up hills.

My name is Nat,
Hyper-active may be
But if you think I'm mad,
You should meet my dad!

My name is Nat,
African plaits no longer,
But still, I'm told,
A big smile.

My name is Nat
And I wish
You all the best
On your wedding day -

I know it sounds cheesy
But I hope and pray
God will bless you
All your days.

Natalie Jagger

Poetic Perambulations

Isn't it wonderful that most of the time,
We can express our thoughts in rhyme.

Rhythm in words for all to see,
Learnt at first from our mother's knee.

Of which close category do they belong?
When can a rhyme become a song?

Deep and meaningful, happy and hunky-dory,
A good poem can take the place of a drawn-out story.

It's a wonderful way of passing the time,
Life is more interesting if you have the rhyme.

Trevor Napper

Flowers At The Door

Flowers at the door, what are they for?
To say that I'm sorry or show that I care,
To let you know I'm thinking of you
Because I'm never there,
I would tell you I'm sorry,
I would show you I care,
I would always be thinking of you,
And always be there.

Kenny Roxburgh